# GUIDANCE AND COUNSELLING
## Educational, Vocational and Career Planning

# Guidance and Counselling

## *Educational, Vocational and Career Planning*

*Edited by*

**G.D. Gururani**

**AKANSHA PUBLISHING HOUSE**

**NEW DELHI - 110 059 (INDIA)**

**AKANSHA PUBLISHING HOUSE**
R-37B, Vani Vihar, Uttam Nagar
New Delhi - 110 059
Email: ektabooks@yahoo.com

*Showroom*
4649/21B, Ansari Road
Daryaganj, New Delhi - 110 002
PHones: 23263193, 9811582579

*Guidance and Counselling*



First Published, 2005
Reprint–2006
Reprint : 2007

ISBN 81-8370-003-9

PRINTED IN INDIA

---

Published by M.P. Misra for Akansha Publishing House, New Delhi - 110 059 and Printed at Tarun Offset Press, Delhi.

To

Dr. S. Radhakrishan

(Former President of India)

A Philosopher-King, a great teacher

this book is humbly dedicated.

# Contents

# Preface

> "The difficulties of life are intended to make us better, not bitter."
>
> —George Gritter

> "No good work whatever can be perfect, and the demand for perfection is always a sign of a misunderstanding of the ends of art."
>
> —John Ruskin

Guidance is counselling or advice on educational, vocational or psychological matters. Commonly it is understood as leadership, instruction or direction. Actually 'guidance' starts from the very beginning at home where parents and elders act as guide for an infant or child. But it is remarkable to note that it cannot be assertained planting a sapling and water it regularly, the direction in which the branches should spread and the thickness of its trunk or even the fruits it bear. Development and growth of personality depends heavily on the kind and quality of guidance one receives at home and later at school and college. Here it must be noted that 'Right Guidance' is necessary for achieving right goals. This means a guide must be well trained professional having deep understanding of child psychology. Generally it is seen that parents want to thrust a career upon their wards. Which is a wrong notion. Under the benevolent care of teacher children blossom and mature. School curriculum is framed on the firm foundation of the genesis and development of human abilities. A variety of disciplines contribute to a holistic cognitive development of children.

Guidance as an organised activity is nascent in India, though it was in vogue in developed western countries since very long. Only recently its need is being felt as such trained professionals are engaged for guidance and counselling at various levels.

Guidance is also necessary for career planning. As such in the modern age of advanced technology career planning is much emphasised. As such a careful and calculated guidance is the need of hour.

The present book gives a vivid account of guidance and counselling—educational, vocational and career planning.

The main topics included in this book are guidance; school curriculum and guidance; guidance in schools; guidance in primary and higher education; training for guidance; mental hygiene and guidance; guidance services; guidance team; towards guidance movement; guidance and evaluation: evolution and development; introduction to counselling; fundamentals of counselling; besides ILO recommendations on guidance principles on vocations etc. The source of information used herein are all secondary e.g. books, abstracts, reports, seminar proceedings, journals etc.

As such the credit for this book goes to different educationists and psychologists whose views are borrowed liberally. I owe a deep sense of gratitude to these men of letters, editors and copyright holders for sharing their research findings.

I am thankful to my teachers and colleagues who have helped me in various ways. My family members and friends deserve my appreciation for their moral support and also for providing congenial work environment at home. Finally, I am thankful to my publisher for publishing this book in superb way.

I will be amply rewarded if this effort will be of some use to those for whom this is meant. Suggestions and constructive criticism from all quarters are welcome to enhance its usefulness.

—GDG

# 1

# Guidance and Counselling

> "My code of life conduct is simply this: work hard, play to allowable limit, disregard equally the good and bad opinions of others; never do a friend a dirty trick; never grow indignant over anything; live the moment to the utmost of its possibilities; and be satisfied with life always, but never with oneself."
>
> —*George Jean Nathan*

Guidance is commonly understood as leadership, instruction or direction. It is counselling or advice on educational, vocational or psychological matters. While the act of guidance is termed as counselling.

The importance of guidance and counselling in educational or vocational purposes was recognised in advanced countries long back. At home in India as an organised activity it is a recent phenomenon—and still in infant stage.

Earlier there was no career planning at all. Exceptions are only there where one aspiring for a certain career achieved the goal with proper planning is pondered over. Though in country where a large number of children are still deprived of basic primary education, there guidance, career planning and other such terms have no meaning. Despite that in the age of globalisation where talents are searched and recruited after undergoing rigorous selection procedure. Very very few opportunities are the while a large army of aspirants is where for. As such the need of guidance and counselling.

# I

It is impossible to think of life without the support one would receive from parents, teachers and friends. In other words we seek informal guidance from those whom we *Trust*. We always seek guidance whenever we encounter a problem that we cannot solve by ourselves. Guidance would be effective only when we *Seek* and not when it is *Offered unasked*. Guidance is a kind of help, assistance, a clarification or a solution to a problem. It implies a state of and helplessness.

**Role of Teacher as Guide**

All teachers guide students whenever the latter approach the former with doubts. That is why a teacher is said to be a "Friend, Philosopher and Guide." A teacher does not solve student's problems. Rather he helps a student to solve his problems himself, so that, in future, whenever he encounters problematic situations he could fall back upon his own resources. Each one is endowed with some "potentialities." Teachers help students transform these "potentialities into "abilities by appropriate guidance and instruction.

**Who is a Counsellor?**

In simple words, one who offers guidance is called a Counsellor. To "Counsel" means to advise or to help. When someone has stomach-pain or fever or headache he approaches a doctor who is a practising physician. When we want to build a house we seek the help of an architect to prepare a plan, a building contractor for execution of construction, a banker to raise a loan. In all these instances we always choose one whom we trust.

A counsellor is one who is "trained" to offer help to students who face problems that they cannot solve themselves. One who receives help is called a Counsellee. "Counselling" refers to the process of helping. The trust or confidence a counsellor has toward a counsellor is termed Rapport. In the absence of rapport, counseling will not be effective. As such it is essential that a counsellor establishes rapport with the student whom he wants to guide.

**Need for Guidance**

All of us have some goals in life. Sometimes the goal on sets for oneself may be unrealistic and beyond reach. Perhaps someone trained in this job would be able to analyse our capabilities and help us set goals that are realistic. We may not be able to meet all needs in the classroom. Beyond classroom also we may have occasions to interact with elders who could guide us. If our resources are not optimally utilised it would be a waste not only for the individual but also for the society to which we belong.

In fact, teachers can act as good guides. Teachers who have been meeting students every day in classrooms, can render assistance to those who need special help. As a matter of fact some teachers do bestow such an individual attention and pupils approach such teachers for help. However, the primary responsibility of a teacher is mainly teaching and evaluation. He needs time for preparation, assessment and also for self-improvement. Therefore, he may not be able to find time to offer this extended service.

**Need of Trained Counsellors**

A trained counsellor may be necessary to perform a variety of services for students in general. One needs to have a good background in Psychology alongwith a Diploma in Educational and Vocational Guidance. A nine-month course in Guidance is being offered at the N.C.E.R.T., New Delhi, leading to a Diploma in Educational and Vocational Guidance. Internship experience in Guidance also forms part of the training programme. Trainees are selected on an All India basis and the candidates are selected on the basis of an Entrance-test and interview. The selected candidates are being offered stipend as well. A trained counsellor administers Psychological Tests like Intelligence tests, Aptitude tests, Personality tests and conducts interviews. Case-studies may be conducted, home-visits undertaken, parental conference organised, conference with other teachers are held and the Counsellor maintains Cumulative Records of all students that contain particulars about scholastic as well as other achievements of pupils. All these responsibilities require a full-time counsellor or more than one counsellor if the students' strength is more. There is an 'apathy' among school administrators to the establishment of a guidance wing to school.

**Types of Guidance**

Some problems stem from subjects one studies and the choice one needs to make at an appropriate stage for further specialisation. There are occasions when one would need guidance to choose an appropriate vocation suited to one's interests, aptitudes and capabilities. One needs to have job-satisfaction. Apart from these specific areas of guidance, students might also need guidance to sort out their personal problems that impede scholastic progress. Unless corrective steps are taken, one would not be able to give of his best in studies.

***1. Educational Guidance***

There has been a phenomenal increase in Teacher-Pupil ratio at the Primary and High-school stages all over the country. Despite earnest efforts most teachers find it a herculean task to attend to the individual needs of children. Since we find a heterogeneous distribution of mental abilities in most classrooms, it becomes difficult for a teacher to adopt different styles of teaching. Particularly below average students lag behind in class-work as they have not been guided to practise good 'study-habits'. Among those, one could also find some who perform low not because their potentialities remain unutilised or underutilised. They are named Underachievers. To quote the recommendation of the Kothari Commission (1964-66).

> "The group of underachievers consists of children who are not intellectually dull, but are atleast of average and may even be of superior ability. The failure of such children should be of great concern to a developing country like ours which cannot remain indifferent to this loss of potential manpower within the higher ability range. Several factors-physical, intellectual, emotional and environmental—contribute to the failure of the underachiever to come up to the level of his latent abilities. The first step is to diagnose the causes of this failure by observation, interrogation and the application of psychological tests, if possible. Such a collection of data will make it possible to have a total appraisal of the situation and indicate lines of remedial treatment.

Despite good intentions parents would not be able to provide a wise counsel. It is clear that it would be beyond the capability of a class-teacher to take up the responsibility of helping pupils cultivate study-habits and analyse their aptitudes so that they could pursue higher studies in the areas where there is a probability of success and satisfaction rather than failure and frustration.

The Kothari Commission have made strong recommendation for the establishment of a Guidance and counselling centre in every school. One of the main functions of the guidance at the secondary level is to aid in the identification and development of the abilities and interests of adolescent pupils. It helps these pupils to understand their own strengths and limitations and to do scholastic work at the level of their ability. It also helps headmaster and teachers to understand their students as individuals and to create situation in which the students can learn more effectively. The role of the counsellor in the promotion of talent can be very important. Where special counsellors are not available, this task will fall on the teachers. It will, therefore, be necessary to train teachers for this responsibility through inservice seminars and special courses. Counsellors help children cultivate good study-habits to optimise their efforts in academic achievement. They also help children identify other interests and hobbies that would add colour to their lives as students. At the end of secondary school stage every student would be baffled at the choices of higher education. Should I go in for Engineering or Medicals or Commerce or Humanities? Invariably such decisions are forced on adolescents by parents. Parents have their own fancy notions regarding higher education. They have little faith in the capacity of their sons and daughters exercising their free-will in this regard. Improper and indiscreet choice of higher education regardless of the aptitudes and interests of learners would spell disaster and ruin the lives of students. The prestige accorded to a few professional courses compels many a parent to push their wards to those colleges, much against their will. A counsellor, who has no vested interest, who neither undervalues nor-overvalues any course of studies would be able to offer wise counsel on the basis of a battery of aptitude tests, intelligence tests interest inventories and individual interviews. It is really unfortunate that even educated parents commit the folly of pushing their sons into Medicals disregarding their poor scholastic performance in Biology and Chemistry. Educational guidance is a must for every student from the viewpoint of long-term interest.

*Principles and Malpractices of Guidance*

*Principle.* Left to themselves and their preceptors students are likely to decide what they should study on the basis of their realistic self-perception.

*Malpractice.* Never trust their capacity to choose because, they are immature. Never allow them to examine their deficiencies. Help them overcome by hook or crook!

*Principle.* Encourage them to approach a teacher on counsellor who would clarify their doubts regarding future and understand their subjects.

*Malpractice.* Send them to a professional tuition-master, trained in the art of 'ramming.' Persuade them reproduce blindly whatever was dictated!

*Principle.* Monetary compensation is secondary. Self-fulfillment is primary. Choose a course of studies or occupation rationally and boldly.

*Malpractice.* The more money you make the higher your status in society. Forget the cliche of job-satisfaction.

*Principle.* Do not hesitate to branch off into Fine Arts if you are talented. Do not blindly join the flock of students gate-crashing into colleges of Medicine and Engineering.

*Malpractice.* You cannot make a living as a musician or a dancer or an artist. You might regret. Never fall into the trap of performing Arts!

**2. *Vocational Guidance***

Broadly, Vocational Guidance is to assist the youths in choosing and preparing for an occupation. The specific aims of Vocational Guidance are:

(i) to assist the pupils to obtain the requisite knowledge about the characteristics and functions of different occupations;

(ii) to give the pupil the necessary opportunities for knowing about different occupational fields even while he/she is in school;

(iii) to help the pupil understand what rewards and personal satisfactions the occupation will provide;

(iv) to enable the pupil to obtain information about the specific skills and abilities required by different occupations such that he/she may make an appropriate choice of an occupation to suit his/her abilities;

(v) to help pupils obtain information about conditions of work in different occupational fields; and

(vi) to save themselves from the experience of being square pegs in round holes.

If Educational Guidance is properly provided and followed the task of the counsellor regarding Vocational Guidance would be to a great extent, simplified. We could identify four stages of development in Vocational awareness among the individuals.

| | | | |
|---|---|---|---|
| (i) | Growth Stage | — | Birth to 14 years. |
| (ii) | Exploratory Stage | — | 15-24 years. |
| (iii) | Establishment Stage | — | 25-44 years. |
| (iv) | Maintenance Stage | — | 45-60 years. |

Counsellor who offers Vocational Guidance is called a Career Master. He would invite successful professionals of different vocations—Medicine, Lawyers, Engineers, Businessmen, Chartered Accountants, Bank Managers etc., to give career—talks' for the benefit of students about to leave the school. They would discuss the scope of the job, complexity of the job, training needed, risks involved, challenges to be faced, and rewards.

A bright probationary officer of a Nationalised Bank was invited to address the students on the employment opportunities in Banking Services. Basically a man of English Literature, he was lured by the emoluments and promotional prospects in Banking and appeared for the competitive examination. Selected and trained for more than four years, he could give a graphic picture of the career-opportunities in Banks. At the end of the talk he confessed in privacy that he did not really enjoy his work. He felt that his talents and capacities were not put to proper use and that he had to do such clerical job that would not warrant high academic qualifications. Is not his placement in a Bank a terrible loss to the academic would. He might have blossomed as an eminent Professor and a creative writer too! When all his energies are sucked and sapped in totalling and tallying and signing, he returns home thoroughly exhausted and disgusted. He becomes a "Cog in the wheel" as Bertrand Russell would put it.

### *3. Personal Guidance*

Personal Guidance is aimed at helping pupils develop interpersonal relationship with their peer-group, overcome minor conflicts and temporary maladjustment. Sometimes children may have differences with parents and this would affect their scholastic performance. Pupils might like to talk to the counsellor some of their personal problems confidentially.

### *Counselling*

Counselling, a process which takes place in an one-to-one relationship between an individual beset by problems which he cannot cope alone, and a professional worker whose training and experience have qualified him/her to help others reach solutions to various degrees of personal difficulties.' Everyone has occasions in life to be shaken, though not shocked, disturbed, though not demoralised; nervous, though not facing a nervous breakdown and a little sad though not sunk in depression. At those agonising moments one would feel the need of timely assistance from someone who can help us to sort out the problem.

Counselling differs from "Psychotherapy." Psychotherapy is concerned with the alleviation of human suffering—the reconstruction of the individual at both the conscious and unconscious levels. Counselling on the other hand, is concerned with aiding "normal" people to achieve better adjustment skills, which manifest themselves in increased maturity, independence, an integrated personality. It is concerned with such problems as "learning difficulties, minor conflicts "involving feelings of anxiety, hostility etc. It has close ties with education. It helps to solve pupils' emotional problems and identify the cause of "Under achievement and failure." It is useful to diagnose learning difficulties and help provide remedies. It aims at "personality growth and development."

*Directive Counselling*

"Directive Counselling" is a process in which the counsellor assumes the major responsibility in solving the problem of the student. The Directive Approach envisages the following steps:

1. Analysis
2. Synthesis
3. Diagnosis
4. Prognosis
5. Counselling
6. Follow-up.

In order to obtain an objective and full understanding, information is collected from cumulative records, autobiographies, anecdotal records and so on. The second step consists of synthesis. Information gathered should be properly analysed and synthesised. No subjective element should be allowed to vitiate the total picture. If the material is not objective, diagnosis may not be reliable. Diagnosis involves identification of the problem and determination of the causes that have led to the problem and searching for relationships, past, present and future, which may help in the understanding of the symptoms. The next step is prognosis. Diagnosis is concerned with the past and present. Prognosis is concerned with the future.

"Counselling" proper is effected through counselling sessions or interviews in which the counsellee is helped to try different solutions to the problems confronting him. No limitations are imposed on the subject regarding the number of solutions he may try. The aim is to enable the subject to try as many solutions as necessary till he is able to reach an optimal solution. The last and the most important step is the "follow-up." The counsellor's interest in the student does not cease with the student finding a solution. The counsellor watches to assess the success or otherwise of the solution reached and the progress of the student.

Directive Counselling stresses the use of 'measurement' and 'prediction.' It is sometimes criticised for being authoritarian.' It assumes, that the subject is 'ignorant' and 'helpless.' The counsellor has the major responsibility for the subject's action. It is a highly 'structured' approach.

The Directive approach outlines five techniques:

(a) Forcing conformity
(b) Changing the environment
(c) Selecting appropriate environment
(d) Learning the needed skills.
(e) Changing attitudes.

***Non-Directive Counselling***

Carl Rogers defines counselling as: "The process by which the structure of the "self" is relaxed in the safety of the client's relationship with the therapist and previously denied experiences are perceived and then integrated into an altered "self."

Rogers views man as "essentially good and rational." He wants to create a psychological climate of "unconditional acceptance " of the individual and help him to "become himself." His book "On Becoming a Person" describes beautifully and lucidly the process of change in human personality. By showing warmth, interest and understanding he helps the subject achieve "Self-realisation." He seldom asks questions. He provides a kind of warmth and emotional support to the patient to talk and analyse his own problems and find a solution himself. To him counselling session in meant for "facilitating the growth of the person." He views man as "Socialised, forward-moving, rational and realistic."

Rogers speaks of a "Fully Functioning Person" when a person sheds off his false front—facade—and understands the core of his personality. Non-directive counselling reinforces faith in an individual that he could solve his problems himself. It certainly takes much more time and patience and tact than directive counselling.

Rogers has definated the following steps.

(i) The client comes for help
(ii) The situation is defined
(iii) The encouragement of free expression
(vi) The counsellor accepts and clarifies
(v) The gradual expression of positive feelings
(vi) The recognition of positive feelings
(vii) The development of insight
(viii) The clarification of choices
(ix) Positive actions
(x) Increasing Insight
(xi) Increased Independence
(xii) The decreased need for help.

***Eclectic Counselling***

Eclectic Counselling is the offshoot of such a search for new method of counselling. Thorne (1950) the exponent of this method, called this the "Integrative "psychology because he attempted to borrow from both. Non directive and directive techniques of counselling. The primary duty of a counsellor is to help the client as best as he can within a time frame. The eclectic approach instead of rigidly employing a particular theoretical principle tries to take the different principles from different theories to suit the individual case and the specific situation. It is a harmonious integration and the most practicable approach to counselling.

**Conclusion**

Therefore, both Guidance and counselling are meant to help individuals to adapt themselves to the world of reality, face the challenges of life with fortitude and thus develop a positive attitude to life.

**Important Guidelines**

(i) To counsel means to render assistance to an individual who faces a problem that he cannot solve by his own effort.

(ii) Teachers have the major responsibility of teaching and evaluation. Hence they may not find adequate time to render specialised guidance services.

(iii) A trained counsellor has adequate expertise to guide students.

(iv) Guidance could be educational, vocational and personal.

(v) Educational guidance helps students to develop proper study habits and also choose courses suited to their aptitudes and interests.

(vi) Vocational guidance informs pupils of the different job opportunities available so that the choice is made rationally and not blindly.

(vii) Directive counselling is prescriptive, structured, methodical wherein the counsellor, takes the major responsibility of guiding and shaping a pupil's behaviour.

(viii) Counselling is a face-to-face contact between a student and a counsellor to discuss and arrive at solutions for personal problems. It is confidential.

(ix) Counselling could be directive, non-directive or eclectic.

(x) Personal guidance promotes interpersonal relations, leading to satisfactory adjustment.

(xi) Non-directive counselling is pupil-centred, informal, unstructured wherein the pupil talks most and arrives at solutions to his problems.

(xii) Midway between the two extremes lies eclectic counselling which is a compromise using the best elements of both directive and non-directive counselling.

## II

## AIM AND SCOPE OF GUIDANCE SERVICES

Guidance services have a much wider scope and function than merely that of assisting students in making educational and vocational choices. The aims of guidance are both adjustive and developmental: it helps the student in making the best possible adjustment to the situations in the educational institution and in the home and at the same time facilitates the development of all aspects of his personality. Guidance, should be regarded as an integral part of education and not a special psychological or social service which is peripheral to educational purposes.

### Guidance in Primary Education

Guidance should begin from the lowest class of the primary school. It can be used in helping pupils to make a satisfactory transition from home to school; in diagnosing difficulties in the learning of basic educational skills; in identifying pupils in need of special education; in helping potential drop-outs to stay in school; in guiding pupils to develop insight into the world of work and favourable attitudes towards work; and in assisting in plans for their further education or training. Little has been done so far in the shape of guidance services at the primary stage because of the large numbers of institutions involved, the poor qualifications of the teachers and the absence of resources. It would, therefore, be unrealistic for a long time to come to think of providing qualified counsellors in these schools. Some guidance functions can, however, be performed by well-trained primary school teachers. Community resources can also be mobilized to meet some of the guidance needs of the young pupils. Suggestions for making a beginning in guidance in the primary school are outlined below:

(i) There should be at least one lecturer in the training school who should be able to deal with the subject of principles of guidance and mental hygiene.

(ii) The training programme for primary school teachers should include acquaintance with simple diagnostic testing, and with the problem of individual differences and their implications for classroom practices.

(iii) Guidance services should be introduced in the training institutions and in schools attached to the institutions so that the trainees may get first-hand knowledge of the problems involved in their organisation.

(iv) Short in-service courses in guidance should be provided for primary school teachers wherever possible.

(v) Simple literature for the occupational orientation of children may be prepared and made available in the regional languages.

(vi) Children and parents should be helped in the selection of courses for further education at the end of the primary stage, and the selection should not be based on the examination results alone.

**Guidance in Secondary Education**

One of the main functions of guidance at the secondary level is to aid in the identification and development of the abilities and interests of adolescent pupils. It helps these pupils to understand their own strengths and limitations and to do scholastic work at the level of their ability to gain information about educational and vocational opportunities and requirements, to make realistic educational and vocational choices and plans based on a consideration of all relevant factors; and to find solutions to their problems of personal and social adjustment the school and the home, Guidance services also help headmasters and teachers to understand their students as individuals and to create situations in which the students can learn more effectively. Following the recommendations of the Secondary Education Commission, the Ministry of Education set up a Central Bureau of Educational and Vocational Guidance in 1954 to give technical advice and help to the nascent guidance movement in the field of secondary education. Guidance became a Centrally sponsored scheme in the Third Plan and 13 Bureaus have now been set up for the development of guidance services in the States. These Central and State-level organisations have developed a modest programme of guidance, and services are rendered to the pupils in the schools by trained counsellors and career masters with the help of the teachers. By the end of the third plan, the number of schools offering some kind of guidance was about 3,000, which constituted only about 13% of the total number of secondary schools in the country. Again the majority of these 3,000 schools have only a career master on the staff and offer only an information service. Very few institutions have a full time or part-time counsellor for giving effective guidance help, including testing and counselling. It is thus clear that although there is an organised movement for providing guidance services in the country, the progress made has been very slow. The ultimate objective should of course be to introduce adequate guidance services in all secondary schools, with a trained counsellor in charge of the programme. Since, however, neither financial allocations nor training facilities for guidance will be available on such a large scale, it is necessary that a short-range programme should be adopted for the next 20 years. The following recommendations are suggested in this regard:

(i) A minimum guidance service should be made available to all secondary schools by having one Visiting School Counsellor for every ten schools located within a reasonable distance of one another, and by allocating the simpler guidance functions to the teachers.

(ii) At the same time, in order to demonstrate what a really comprehensive guidance service is like and what it can achieve, it would be desirable to set up comprehensive guidance services in a few carefully selected schools, preferably one in each district.

(iii) The necessary supervisory staff to inspect and offer consultation to the school workers should be appointed in the State Bureau of Guidance.

It is the need of the hour that all secondary school teachers should be given some understanding of guidance concepts and simple guidance techniques as a part of the programme intended for every trainee. Special or advanced courses should be provided for those who wish to study the subject in depth. Every training college should have on its staff a person having at least the training considered essential for school counsellors. Provision should also exist for the in-service training of the training college staff in guidance and counselling. Adequate arrangements should be made for the professional training of guidance workers. The training of career masters may be undertaken by the State Bureaux as well as the training colleges with the collaboration of the vocational guidance officers of the National Employment

Service. Professional courses of longer duration should be offered by the universities. As the number of persons capable of conducting training programmes for guidance workers is extremely limited, higher level training programmes in guidance to prepare qualified guidance workers to undertake training and research should be initiated at the national level.

**Talent Search and Development**

*Significance:* A dearth of competent and trained manpower is now felt in nearly every branch of national life, and is probably one of the biggest bottlenecks to progress. Poor as we are financially, the poverty of trained intellect is still greater. We might do well to remember.

Native intelligence is generally distributed equitably throughout the population. If it is duly discovered and developed, our large population can be our most valuable asset. Abysmally, very little of the available talent is now discovered and developed.

(i) In a large majority of the homes, the environment is depreciatory on account of the illiteracy of the parents and poverty, and does not allow the available native talent to develop itself fully.

(ii) A good deal of potential talent never enters school. At the primary stage, the proportion of children not enrolled varies from 10% to 60% in different areas. Even among those who enter, about 40% are eliminated in class I itself and only about 25% belonging to about the top 20% of families in the society, complete primary education. Secondary education is largely a privilege of the top 10% of the families and higher education of the 5%.

(iii) Even the talent that enters school and succeeds in climbing the educational ladder does not flower fully because it is not discovered sufficiently early and is often studying in poor schools. For obtaining the best results in quality, talent has to be located early and allowed to grow in the best atmosphere and under the best teachers.

(iv) To determine talent by considering total marks obtained in an examination is a very ineffective method. The highly gifted students are far too creative to be confined within the perimeters of classroom instruction, textbooks and examinations. The genius in one field is generally poor in several others and, in our examination system, a genius is more likely to fail or put up only a mediocre 'total' of marks than to come out at the top. Such search separately for each especial talent, whether in mathematics, science, literature, fine arts, sports or technology and engineering.

As talent is the most valuable asset a country can have, the returns will be immense. Moreover, the search for talent must be a continuous process and has to be taken up at all stages. The secondary stage, however, is the most crucial; and a reference has already been made to the manner in which universities can help in the identification of gifted students at this stage and help them to develop.

The provision of five years of good and effective primary education to every child will enable the country to cast its net for talent to the widest extent possible. The large programme of scholarships proposed at all stages will ensure that all gifted students, or at least the top 5-15% of the relevant age-group, will be enabled to receive the highest education possible. The placement programme which we suggest will also make it possible for them to study in the best institutions available at each stage. In addition to these programmes, it is also necessary to introduce enrichment programmes for the brighter students in as many schools as possible and ultimately in every school. The performance of talented students in the enrichment programmes should be recorded in special certificates which will indicate to the colleges or other institutions of higher education their special abilities and attainments. Care should be taken to ensure that the enrichment programmes do not degenerate into coaching for passing examinations with higher marks. The flexibility in the school curriculum that we have proposed in the preceding chapter would enable the schools to provide enriched or advanced courses for the talented and help them to progress at their own speed. This will also release time for teachers to help the average and backward students. A variety of extra-mural programmes can also be organised for the talented students, either separately by each school or by schools acting in cooperation or by the Education Departments.

Some suggest measure can be:

(i) A five to six-week summer vacation programme can be arranged for a group of academically talented children, from different schools, brought together to an educational centre having special facilities of staff, library, laboratory and equipment. The programme may be renewed for the particular, group from year to year, so that the students get an opportunity to develop their special talent over a number of years.

(ii) Well-planned visits may be arranged to laboratories, museums, and other places.

(iii) Talented students may be brought into contact with persons engaged in the types of work for which the students show special ability or interest. These persons may be able to provide occasional opportunities for the students to work in their special fields.

(iv) Hostels or Day Centres may be made available for those students whose home environment is not conducive to proper study.

The development of the emotional and social aspects of his personality, and of socially desirable attitudes, is also very important. In planning for the development of the talented student, it should be remembered that it is not only his intellectual competence or special ability that needs to be developed.

The role of the counsellor in the promotion of talent can be very important. The counsellor with his detailed knowledge of each talented student is in a unique position to formulate a programme of enrichment for him and to suggest the necessary modifications in the curricular and extra-curricular requirements. Where special counsellors are not available, this task will fall on the teachers. It will, therefore, be necessary to train teachers for this responsibility through in-service seminars and special courses. It should be impressed on them that the classroom atmosphere and the attitudes of teachers is of considerable importance. In a social and educational set-up like ours where the relationship between the teacher and the taught is still largely authoritarian, the general tendency is to suppress any urges and interests that deviate from the class room. The first requirement for the promotion of talent, therefore, is for the teachers to create an atmosphere of free expression in the classroom and to provide opportunities for creative work.

**Education of the Backward Child**

With the rapid expansion of educational facilities, the number of backward children in schools is also increasing. Many of them drop out of schools at one stage or another, either because of their inability to satisfy the academic standards or the boredom and frustration they feel in the pursuit of an academic programme which is largely unrelated to their needs and interests. Though quite a few of these children manage to enter high school or even college, their performance continues to be very poor.

### *Types of Backwardness*

Backwardness is largely due to one of two reasons which sometimes overlap: (1) mental handicap or low intelligence, arising from hereditary or congenital factors or disease or injury; (2) under-achievement or inability to perform up to the level of one's intelligence, especially in persons intellectually well endowed, frequently due to emotional conflict, lack of motivation, poor study habits, cultural deprivation and economic handicaps. On the basis of studies made in educationally advanced countries, it is estimated that 75% of the backward children belong to the first category, usually referred to as the mentally handicapped, and the remaining 25% belong to the second category, usually designated as the under-achievers. In our case, the latter category would be obviously much greater. Both these categories of pupils, for different reasons, are unable to profit from normal education.

### Guiding Mentally Charged

The mentally handicapped are generally classified into four groups: the idiots; the imbeciles; the educable mentally handicapped morons; and the dull or slow-learners. The first three groups of backward children, who have an intelligence quotient below 75, cannot benefit from formal education in ordinary classes. Suitable provision should, however, be made for the education of the dull, who on account of their slower rate of mental development, cannot learn at the ordinary pace of normal children.

In the ordinary classes, where instruction is traditionally geared to the needs of the average child, the dull have to work under a great hardship. They need individual attention, special remedial help and probably also a modified curriculum to suit their rate of learning. In big cities, it may be possible to establish special schools for them as has been done in some educationally advanced countries, but in most cases, special classes in the ordinary schools and individual tuition to the extent possible are the only general remedy.

**Guiding Underachievers**

The group of under-achievers consists of children who are not intellectually dull, but are at least of average and may even be of superior ability. The failure of such children should be of great concern to a developing country like ours, which cannot remain indifferent to this loss of potential manpower within the higher ability range. Several factors—physical, intellectual, emotional and environmental—contribute to the failure of the under-achiever to come up to the level of his latent abilities. The first step is to diagnose the causes of this failure by observation, interrogation and the application of psychological tests, if possible. Such a collation of data will make it possible to have a total appraisal of the situation and indicate lines of remedial treatment. Once the child's errors and difficulties are located, a remedial programme should be formulated and carried out.

The remedial programme should aim at correcting the basic errors, raising his attainment level in the subject or subjects, re-establishing his confidence in himself and in his ability to succeed, and creating for him new interest and motivation in his studies. The remedial measures should involve the student himself as much as possible and should be organised individually or in small groups. The assessment of the student's progress should be made not against any external standards but with reference to his own previous performance. Remedial programmes are particularly needed in reading, spelling and number work in the earlier stages, and in language and computational skills in the later stages. Since these educationally retarded children are not underachieving because of innate low mental capacity, their needs can be met by remedial arrangements within the school system. What the student requires is help for a limited period and within a limited area of study. This may be done by assigning the responsibility to one or two interested teachers during specific periods in the week. Remedial groups could be set up after school hours, two or three days in the week, with subject experts in charge of each group.

Guidance and counselling services have an important role to play in the education of the backward, especially with regard to identification of the group, diagnosis of their special defects and planning for their education and future occupation. But these services, have not been developed and the programme has to be carried on with whatever help and guidance can be given by teachers in the school. The essential factor for success of the programme is the coordinated approach that the entire school faculty should make to the problem of these children with a degree of sympathy and understanding and with an insight into child psychology born out of long experience. The teacher should ordinarily be able to give some help to the under-achievers. Parent-teacher associations should be mobilized for enlisting the co-operation of parents in dealing with special cases. It is necessary, however, that there should be at least one child guidance clinic in each major town, and it should be adequately manned.

**Teachers' Evaluation Programme**

The baneful effects of the system on education in general, and secondary education in particular, have been discussed in the reports of several committees and commissions. The Secondary Education Commission after reviewing these defects at the secondary education stage, recommended a new approach to school evaluation and made a number of concrete proposals for the improvement of the external examination and the methods of internal assessment. As a result of these proposals, a movement was started for examination reform, which gathered momentum with the establishment of the Central Examination Unit of trained evaluation officers by the Government of India in 1958. The outstanding feature of the new reform movement is the emphasis laid on the modern concept of evaluation.

*The New Concept*

Evaluation is a continuous process which forms an integral part of the total system of education, and is intimately related to educational objectives. It exercises a great influence on the pupil's study habits and the teacher's methods of instruction and thus helps not only to measure educational achievement but also to improve it. The techniques of evaluation are means of collecting evidence' about the student's development in desirable directions. These techniques should, therefore, be valid, reliable, objective and practicable. As the common method of evaluation used at present in India is the written examination, a natural corollary of the acceptance of the new approach will be to improve the written examination in such a way that it becomes a valid and reliable measure of educational achievement. There are, however, several important aspects of the student's growth that cannot be measured by written examinations, and other methods such as observation techniques, oral tests and practical examinations, have to be devised for collecting evidence for the purpose.

The Central Examination Unit has worked with thousands of secondary school teachers in seminars and workshops, introduced hundreds of training college lecturers to the new techniques, established a very large pool of test items, trained paper-setters attached to different Boards of Secondary Education, published a good deal of literature on evaluation and carried out or sponsored several studies and investigations on various practical problems in examinations. As the work of the Unit expanded, the Government of India approved of the establishment of Evaluation Units in different States during the Third Plan period. But the task is a stupendous one, and it will take considerable time for the new measures to make their impact on objectives, learning experiences and evaluation procedures in school education. The improvements already made in the external examination by the different Boards have not removed all its major defects. The objectives have not yet been enlarged to include the testing of application and problem-solving abilities. The character of the school examinations, at least in the senior classes, is determined largely by that of the external examination, and the new techniques of evaluation are not readily adopted in these internal examinations. Besides this all the efforts in the direction of reform have been confined to the field of secondary education.

One of the main purposes of evaluation at the primary stage is to help the pupils improve their achievement in the basic skills and to develop the right habits and attitudes with reference to the objectives of primary education. These objectives and their implications for evaluation should be made clear to the teachers. It would be desirable to treat the lower primary stage covering classes I to IV as an ungraded unit, because this would help the children coming from different backgrounds to advance at their own pace.

The two-year block may be divided into two groups, one for slow-learners and the other for fast-learners to enable different pupils to proceed at the level of their ability and move from one unit to another. Such a division, however, will be practicable only in a large-size school with more than one section in each class. If the experiment regarding the ungraded unit succeeds in classes I and II, it may be extended to the remaining classes of the lower primary stage. Teachers should be prepared for the ungraded system through the regular training courses and orientation programmes and should be helped with a supply of diagnostic tests and remedial material. The orientation may be given by the State Institutes of Education. Observation techniques, which are more reliable for assessing the pupil's growth at this stage than mere formal techniques, of evaluation, should be used by teachers in a planned and systematic manner.

Currently evaluation in high primary classes is carried out largely by means of written examinations. Due importance should be given here also to oral tests, which should form a part of the internal assessment. The teacher should be helped in such assessment with a rich supply of evaluation materials prepared by the State Evaluation Organisations, including standardized achievement tests. Diagnostic testing is necessary here and indeed throughout the school stage. In most causes, such testing will be through simple teacher-made diagnostic tests. Cumulative record cards play a vital role in indicating the growth and development of the pupil at each stage, his academic and emotional problems, and his difficulties of adjustment, if any, and the directions in which remedial action is to be taken to solve his problems or difficulties. We are of the opinion that cumulative record cards intended for the primary classes should be very simple, so that primary teachers can use them with just a little training. In the first instance, the cards should be introduced from class IV onwards in about 10% of selected schools as an experimental measure; but once the majority of teachers are trained in evaluating certain important aspects of the child's personality and the proper maintenance of the records, the use of the cards may be gradually extended to all the higher primary and, as a next step, even to lower primary schools. An external examination at the end of the primary stage (class VII or VIII) to be taken compulsorily by all pupils was strongly recommended by some witnesses who appeared before the Commission. It was pointed out that an external examination was necessary for:

(i) maintaining certain uniform standards at the end of the stage;

(ii) providing a basis for choice of courses at the secondary stage; and

(iii) creating incentives for better teaching and learning.

But all these arguments do not establish a case for an external examination of the formal type to be compulsorily taken by all the pupils in class VII or VIII. The first national standard of attainment should be defined at the end of the primary stage, it is unnecessary to prescribe a rigidly uniform level of attainment for all the primary school pupils in a State or even in a district, through an external examination. Further, instead of creating incentives for better teaching, the external examination intended for all will saddle teachers with standardized programmes and encourage the process of rote memorisation, which is the besetting evil of teaching and learning methods in our schools today.

By making use of the standardized or refined test material referred to above, the district educational authorities may, if they so desire, arrange for a common examination to be taken by the pupils of all the schools in a district at the end of the primary stage. This common school leaving examination will be different from the school certificate examination now held in many States, because though the question papers will be set by the district educational authorities or by special paper-setters appointed by the State Evaluation Organisation, the performance of the pupils of each participating school will be assessed by the teachers of the school themselves, and not by external examiners. The advantages of such a common final examination for the primary schools are obvious. As the question papers will contain standardized tests and highly refined and professional test items, the evaluation will be more valid and reliable than what is possible through the kind of annual and final examinations conducted in the ordinary primary school. Moreover, through such common tests inter-school comparability with regard to levels of performance in the district can be obtained, and this would be helpful, as shown above, both to the education officers and to the schools.

It should be to emphasised that the question papers in the different subjects at this common examination should be of short duration, each of not more than one hour or one hour and a half, so that the entire examination should be completed in two or three days. The whole purpose of the proposal is to reform the existing examination by making it less formal, reducing its burden on the pupils' minds, and increasing its validity as a measure of educational attainment. The school at the primary stage plays the determining role in the total assessment of such attainment. The certificate regarding the completion of the course should be given by the school and not by the external agency, and this certificate should be accompanied by a statement showing the results of the common final examination, if any, together with the results of the internal assessment made by the school of the pupils' performance throughout the year, as shown in his cumulative records. In addition to the common examination, special tests may be held at the end of the primary course for the award of scholarships or certificates of merit or for the purpose of identifying talent and pupils may appear for these tests on a voluntary basis.

As per practice, currently the external examination in the case of the higher secondary class or the intermediate classes located in the school, the external examination is held by the State Board of Secondary (or Higher Secondary) Education and in the case of pre-university class, by the university concerned.

It is to be noted here in this connection that:

(i) Most of the drawbacks in the present system of external examinations are due to defective questions and the question papers set for the examination. The paper-setters are, by and large, appointed on the basis of seniority, subject competence, and experience in teaching. Hardly few of them possess the necessary knowledge and skill in the construction of valid and reliable tests. No major breakthrough towards the improvement of external examinations is possible unless (a) the technical competence of paper-setters is raised through an intensive training programme sponsored by the State Boards; (b) the question papers are oriented to testing not merely the acquisition of knowledge but the ability to apply knowledge and the development of problem-solving abilities; and (c) the nature of the questions asked is improved.

(ii) Besides the improvement of questions and question papers, many other procedures of the external examinations need to be made more systematic and scientific. For example, the marks of different subjects are added without being standardized. The determination of cut-off points, the award of grace marks and other similar methods are also not based on any sound rationale. All these factors tend to make the examinations scores less and less reliable. It is essential that scientific scoring procedures should be devised so that there may be optimum reliability in the assessment of the candidate's performance.

(iii) With the rapidly-increasing number of students appearing for the Board examinations, the task of getting the answer scripts properly valued and of processing the results efficiently within a stipulated time is becoming more and more difficult. It is necessary that this process should be mechanized so as to make it more accurate and expeditious.

**Experimental Schools**

In order to lessen its importance still further, a few selected schools should be given the right of assessing their students themselves and holding their own final examination at the end of class X, which will be regarded at equivalent to the external examination of the State Board of School Education. The State Board will issue the certificates to the successful candidates of these schools on the recommendation of the schools. A committee set up by the State Board of School Education should develop carefully worked-out criteria for the selection of such schools. The schools should not only be freed from the requirements of an external examination but should be permitted to frame their own curricula, prescribe their own textbooks, and conduct their educational activities without departmental restrictions. This is a bold step in the direction of freedom and of educational experimentation. But the right given to the experimental schools should be reviewed periodically as institutions invested with such powers should continuously earn their privilege.

**Internal Assessment**

The internal assessment or evaluation conducted by individual schools is of great significance and should be given increasing importance. It should be comprehensive, evaluating all those aspects of the student's growth that are measured by the external examination and also those personality traits, interests and attitudes which cannot be assessed by it. Internal assessment should be built into the total educational programme of the school and should be used for improvement rather than for certifying the level of achievement of the student. It must be pointed out that all items of internal assessment need not follow qualified scoring procedures. Some of them may be assessed in descriptive terms. The results should be kept separately and not be combined artificially with other results to form aggregate scores. The written examinations conducted in schools should be improved on the same lines as the external examination. There is need for developing other types of evaluation tools for improving internal assessment such as interest inventories, aptitude tests and rating scales. They should be prepared by specialists and made available to schools, and the teachers should be trained to use them through a network of in-service programmes. Teachers should also be trained to make simple tests of their own on the models supplied and use them for the assessment of the performance of their pupils. The experience of introducing internal assessment has not been very happy so far and that there has been persistent over-assessment by the weaker schools. This has led some critics to suggest that the system should be abandoned altogether. Internal assessment has to continue and its importance will have to be increasingly emphasized.

It is very apt to follow the following:

(i) The internal assessment and external examination results should not be combined because the purposes and techniques of the two evaluations are different and because the results of the internal assessment of the different institutions are not strictly comparable. The results of the external and internal assessment should, therefore, be shown separately in the certificates given at the end of the course.

(ii) It should be taken due note of while classifying the schools and should also be related to grants-in-aid so that institutions which tend to over-assess their students persistently would stand to lose in status and finance. The grant-in-aid rules should also authorize the Education Department to withdraw recognition for persistent irresponsible assessment.

The continual deepening of the curricula should be accompanied by an equally vigorous improvement in the method of teaching and evaluation. The main factors responsible for the dull and uninspiring school teaching today are the rigidity of the educational system and the failure of the administrative machinery to diffuse new educational practices to schools. These weaknesses should be overcome.

### *Elasticity and Dynamism*

A good educational system should be dynamic, flexible and discriminating enough to help institutions and teachers to proceed along different levels of development—the good schools be free to go ahead on creative and experimental lines while the weaker ones should be supported to gain a sense of security. Such elasticity and dynamism are possible if the experimenting teacher is supported by the administrative authority, a general atmosphere of reform, the encouragement of the head of the institution, a mastery of subject-matter, leadership provided by training institutions, and the availability of teaching materials. Elasticity in a school system will have little value if hew practices developed are not diffused to schools and teachers given skilled help in trying out innovations.

*Textbooks, teachers' guides and materials:* Provision of quality textbooks and other teaching-learning materials is a key programme for raising standards at comparatively low cost. A comprehensive programme of textbook production at the national level should be implemented by mobilising the best talent in the country on the lines already being attempted by NCERT. Such books will facilitate the definition and practical indication of expected standards. They will also help in national integration. The Ministry of Education should take steps to establish in the public sector an autonomous organisation, functioning on commercial lines for the production of textbooks at the national level, especially scientific and technical books. A small committee may be set up to work out the details of the project. The effort at the national level should be supported and augmented by each State setting up an expert section for the production of textbooks. The preparation, try-out and evaluation of textbooks should be the responsibility of the State Education Departments. The production aspect of the textbooks may preferably be done by the State Education Departments, wherever possible, through their own textbook presses. The sale and distribution of textbooks are better left to the student cooperatives and not be assumed directly by the Departments.

The production of textbooks and teaching aids at the State level should preferably be entrusted to an autonomous agency functioning in close liaison with the Education Department. The machinery set up should be such that the textbooks are subjected to continuous revision and improvement. At least 3 or 4 books should be provided in each subject to provide a multiple choice of books for the schools. Liberal policies should be adopted for remunerating authors. The entire organisation of State production of textbooks should be run on a no-profit-no-loss basis. Manuscripts should be invited from a variety of sources including teachers, and a high-level committee of professional persons should select and approve manuscripts. Teachers' guides and other instructional material should supplement textbooks. Lists of minimum teaching aids and equipment needed by each category of schools should be prepared and steps taken to provide the equipment to every school on a high priority basis. Education Departments should work with the All-India Radio for the use of radio lessons, supplemented by printed guide materials for teachers and pupils. Broadcasting of special 'radio talks specially designed for teachers in the mornings and evenings will help teachers in lesson preparation. Sophisticated forms of newer techniques would not be suitable at present in the general run of schools but may be tried out experimentally in teacher-training institutions. Teachers should be helped and trained to rely on inexpensive and locally available or improvised teaching aids. Costly equipment should be shared by schools in a neighbourhood.

**Size of Class**

Classes of somewhat larger size than what is strictly considered as desirable cannot be avoided in India for a long time. However, it is necessary to restrict the number of pupils admitted to each class to a maximum of 50 in the lower primary, 45 in the higher primary and lower secondary, and 40 in higher secondary classes. Research should be undertaken in the problems and techniques of multiple-class teaching. Training institutions should orient teachers to these techniques.

**Guidance and Counselling**

Guidance and counselling should be regarded as an integral part of education, meant for all students and aimed at assisting the individual to make decisions and adjustments from time to time.

(i) *Guidance, at the primary stage.* Guidance should begin from the lowest class in the primary school and in view of the large numbers of schools involved, the programme may be introduced through simple measures such as:

  (a) familiarising teachers under training with diagnostic testing and the problem of individual differences;

  (b) organising in-service courses for primary teachers;

  (c) producing occupational literature; and

  (d) helping pupils and parents in choice of further education.

(ii) *Guidance at the secondary stage.* Guidance at the secondary stage should, among other things, help in the identification and development of the abilities and interests of adolescent pupils. The ultimate objective should be to introduce adequate guidance services in all secondary schools with a trained counsellor in charge of the programme. But in view of the limited financial and personnel resources, a short-range programme should be adopted for the next 20 years consisting of:

(a) a minimum guidance programme for all secondary schools through a visiting school counsellor for a group often schools, assisted by the school teachers in the simpler guidance functions;

(b) comprehensive guidance programme in selected schools, one in each district, to serve as models; and

(c) provision of necessary supervisory staff in the State Bureaux of Guidance.

# 2

# School Curriculum and Guidance

> "A wise man will so act that whatever he does may rather seem voluntary and of his own free will than done by compulsion, however much he may be compelled by necessity."
>
> —*Niccolo Machiavelli*

When, after twelve years of following the available curricula in the public schools today, a young graduate takes inventory of exactly what saleable product his training gives him, a mental state of bewilderment is frequently the only definite reaction of which he is certain. Because New York State does cover so representative a cross section of the country's population, the results and conclusions of the recent comprehensive study into the "Character and Cost of Education" which has been carried on there are significant for teachers and guidance workers from Canada to Mexico, and from the Atlantic to the Pacific. Dr. Gulick, in commenting on this investigation, as reported by the daily press, holds that the investigators, all of whom were sufficiently able to have achieved national reputations, found that New York schools, although equal to and in some instances better than those of other states, were turning out graduates unready for adult life.

Dr. Gulick maintains that the findings of the inquiry justify the statement that New York's vocational-school programme is too highly specialised in specific trades to meet the needs of youth under modern industrial conditions. He painted the following picture of average school graduates:

> They have no idea what work means; what sort of opportunities there are; how to look for work, or how to work when they get a job. They are not prepared to be useful citizens, or to enter community or home life. They do not know how to take care of their bodies or minds. Few have implanted in them any seeds of individual inner life or growth; any skill in working with others; or any protection against mob hysteria, propaganda, shallow prejudices, or economic gold bricks.

There seems to be an impenetrable wall of sacredness about the public-school curriculum which makes any who would tamper with the status quo an intellectual outlaw and an academic heretic. Yet, if asked the purpose of the curriculum, perhaps even the most conservative of educators would reply that the curriculum is a programme of studies designed to prepare the individual student for life, If such is their answer, the following two questions, if honestly answered, should lead even the most conservative educational thinker to conclude that curriculum changes are in order. Is it not true that the academic curriculum in use today is essentially the same as that in vogue thirty years ago? If so, is the life for which students are preparing the same as the life for which students were preparing thirty years ago? The answer to this question is plainly "No." Today a high-school education is an expected experience for a practically non-selected intelligence range of youth, whereas thirty years ago such was not the case. Hence, the life for which the majority of high-school students are preparing is not the same type of life as that for which the students of thirty years ago were preparing and for which the curriculum was originally designed.

Perhaps there is no one in the school system better prepared to speak of the type of ability trends shown by the students, and of the functional occupational areas for which they must be trained in life, than the counselor whose job it is to know, as far as it is possible to know, these two bodies of facts. Hence, to the extent that current conditions merit different types of life preparation, each counselor in each community situation is confronted with the task of designing and installing courses which are the answer to the life-adaptation needs of the students.

From a broad point of view there are some curricular changes for the general high-school group which the accumulated counselling experience of the authors leads them to suggest:

1. Students whose I.Q.'s are under 115 and who are not going to college are going to be faced with the duties of Voting and of citizenship just as really as the genius is faced by them. A series of major courses in basic economics, civics, and government, not only American but European and Asiatic as well, is here recommended as a four-year required unit. Such a series should be education's answer to the "isms" which find such fertile field in minds not fortified by knowledge. The nation's regard for the citizenship that it bestows on its youth should be such as to insure for these "citizens-to-be" the best preparation for that citizenship that is now available, not in the form of a minor elective course, but as a series of well-planned major required courses. If the objection is raised that the curriculum is already too full, it is possible that there is greater argument in favor of these courses in fundamental economics, civics, and government for the I.Q. range below 115 than there is for some of the required mathematics and foreign-language courses now in some school curricula.
2. A second curricular change which seems to deserve

recommendation is that most trade schools as such should be expanded to include occupational-area training, and that those occupations in which students' functional training can be utilised be constantly impressed on them. The need for research here is both recognised and recommended. At this time, any functional occupational breakdown is an arbitrary one. The one offered is arbitrary, and is there recommended as a beginning point only in the sincere hope that sound research will replace every arbitrary phase.

3. For this same I.Q. group, which of course includes all save approximately 15 per cent of the students in high school, we also recommend a four-year major required course on the human mind and body. This course should include not only fundamental physiology, hygiene, and health knowledge, but also the fundamentals of psychology as they are related to the art of successfully living together. These students, regardless of their I.Q., have bodies which need care; most of them will have homes and all of them will have continuing human relationships. There are certain fundamentals in physiology, psychology, and health hygiene which they need to know, perhaps even more than they need to know who won the Peloponnesian Wars. We do not advocate the sacrificing of ancient history, foreign language, or mathematics. If, after the students in this I.Q. group have been prepared fur life as they will live it as far as modern knowledge can prepare them, there is still time for languages, mathematics, and ancient history, by all means let these courses remain. But first things should be put first. Certainly a country as rich in natural resources as the United States, which is unable to rid itself of an economic depression in eight years, needs a more completely economically

> informed electorate. Further, in a country where freedom in the choice of a mate is the custom, and yet where three of every ten of those choices end in broken homes, greater emphasis should be placed on a more complete knowledge of the forces basic to human relationships.

Obviously, the courses suggested above are recommended as required courses for every student who is not going to college, regardless of his occupational sphere. The functional occupational-area training is suggested as an approach rather than the present specific-trades approach, because every individual should be trained for as broad a life as he is capable of living, and there are very few individuals whose capacity tendencies cannot be effectively utilised in several occupations containing common functional areas. When out of a job, the individual whose sole training has been trade-school preparation for one job probably will feel that he must either find that one job for which he is trained or seek day labor or relief; whereas the individual who has been given proficiency in a functional occupational area and has lost a job will not feel the need of seeking either unskilled labor or relief until every phase of his functional occupational area has been tried. When he is out of a job in one phase, the knowledge given in school of other occupations which require the same functional work will aid him in intelligently seeking another job. The originating and promoting of curricular changes to meet students' changing life needs is a logical and natural outgrowth of the counselor's duties.

Recognition of the problems, not only of youth but of all human kind, is also leading educators to lay emphasis in the preparation of this forward-looking curriculum upon a positive and constructive approach to problems rather than upon a negative and destructive approach. For example, it is not impossible that emphasis within the histories of the future will be upon cultural and economic advances of mankind rather than upon horrors, plagues, and wars. It is possible that the Pasteurs of the future will receive more pages in the history books of the future than will the Napoleons. It is even probable that the school curricula of the future will take into account the extent of world and of individual unhappiness, misunderstanding, and hatred, recognizing that such conditions are prevalent because human beings haven't learned how to live with one another. An outgrowth of this realisation may well be basic courses in ethics and practical psychology, even for children in the elementary schools.

The problem of devising proper curricula for individuals of vastly different receptive powers — the curricula to supply information of varying kinds and degrees of difficulty, in a changing economic order — is one of the big problems the counselor must aid in solving. The counselor with his comprehensive picture of the unique needs of the individual members of the student body, together with his knowledge of current work areas, is in a strategic position to *"see first"* new curricula needs. The counselor's continuing question must be *where* are workers most needed, and *'when* will they be needed? Further, what kind of-*work operations* and what kind of *ability* does this most likely work situation indicate? The machine-tool industries would not now be without sufficient trained mechanics had the curricula makers of four years ago formulated their curricula in terms of workers' age distributions, saturation of employment, and individual aptitudes.

In other words, a study of the workers on the job would have revealed that the average age of machine-tool mechanics was beyond that of the average industrial worker. Immediately such a finding should have been a signal meaning, "Train reinforcements for this work area," and students who evidenced mechanical proficiency should have been given an opportunity to be trained accordingly.

**Towards a Practical Approach**

A part of the counselor's task is to find inventive minds and to direct them toward their opportunities. In the following chapter the place of a study of *inventions* in the curriculum will be discussed. Today the average age of workers in the railroad industry is beyond that of the average industrial worker, and unless steps are taken to train more railroad workers, about four years from now, despite the present decline in the industry, there probably will be a shortage of workers similar to that now existing in the machine-tool industry. The counselor must be alert to such current employment information. Intelligent use of it may be of much value not only to the counselor but to the industries concerned.

Two kinds of industrial information are indicated here as being helpful for curricular planning: (i) existent states of growth and decline within the industry, and (ii) existent conditions within the industry which may lead to a need for increasing or decreasing the number of workers currently employed or replacing them. Dr. A.F. Hinrichs gives an example of the type of industrial information, regarding existing states of growth and decline within the industry, which should be helpful to every counselor:

> There are a limited number of examples of manufacturing industries in which employment declined substantially between 1929 and 1937. To start with [the cigar industry], which dropped 28,000 people. This reflects an absolute decline in the number of cigars smoked and a rapid introduction of machine processes for hand processes. There is no reason to expect that there will ever again be as many people employed in the manufacture of cigars as were employed in 1929. The trend may very well continue down. Silk and rayon employed 13,500 less workers in 1937 than in 1929. The silk industry has been declining and will probably continue to decline. Rayon can be handled with fewer workers than equal quantities of silk.

. . . [The tire and tube industry] dropped 20,000 people, reflecting fundamental and almost revolutionary changes in both the process of producing tires and in the life of the tires produced.

These seem to be the outstanding examples of net losses in employment attributable largely to technological shifts. There are three industries in which substitution has accounted for very substantial losses of employment. The first of these is manufactured ice, from which industry 13,500 people were dropped between 1929 and 1937. Somewhere near this number of people appear to have been added in the manufacture of electric refrigerators.

We cannot account as definitely for declines of 19,000 wage earners in the furniture and wood turning industries, of 7,300 in the production of rubber boots and shoes, of 7,100 in men's and women's hats and millinery, and of 6,800 in silverware, plated ware and jewellery. There has been an absolute decline in the production of rubber boors and shoes. This may very well be connected with changes in our habits of living as induced by the automobile. The change in the furniture industry may be related to the lack of development of new homes as well as to some shift in consumer preferences....

... In order to make the list complete, I should perhaps add cotton textiles, employing an average of 435,400 in 1937 and 441,100 in 1929. The decline, much smaller relatively than in the other industries listed, is large in absolute terms and accounts for more than 5,000 workers. Here then are possibly 139,000 jobs that disappeared on the basis of net changes between 1929 and 1937. . . .

Looking look at the other side of the picture. We are frequently told that what is needed in the United States is a new industry. Did any new industries develop between 1929 and 1937? The Census gives evidence of only two industries in 1937 that employed as many as 10,000 workers which were essentially nonexistent in 1929. 62,000 additional people were employed in the manufacture of alcoholic beverages of one sort or another. Virtually none had been legally so employed in 1929. Nearly 17,000 people were employed in the manufacture of synthetic resins and plastics. Only 3,500 workers Were classified in this industry by the Census in 1929. Because of a change in classification of the industry in 1931, the figure of 3,500 workers in 1929 is not exactly comparable to the figure of 17,000 in 1937. If the data could be made comparable, the increase in employment in the industry would be somewhat smaller than 13,500.

Five industries, however, experienced an increase of employment of more than 40 percent between 1929 and 1937. While none of them may be regarded as a new industry, they are certainly indicating rates of growth sufficiently large to meet the desire that is expressed when we say that we need new industries in the United States. These industries were canning, which added 43,000 workers; stamped and pressed metal ware, 21,000; rayon production, 16,000; aircraft, 9,000; and asbestos products, used largely for insulation, 5,000. There was a total growth in these five industries of 94,000 workers.

The counselor who attempts to counsel and to advise in curricular foundation without such information is unfair to students.

There is a shortage of the second type of study above indicated—namely, studies of existing conditions within individual industries and their relations to general employment conditions. Recognizing this shortage, college curricula makers might well add courses which would train analytically minded students to make such studies. For those guidance workers in school systems in which no provision is made for such studies and who, therefore, must make their own, we outline here the following practical procedures.

1. From the United States Bureau of Labor Statistics obtain the average total number of functionally classified workers employed per industry and in all industries per year for the preceding ten-year period. The average for all industries, adjusted for changes in the population, should be close to the average total number to be employed during the next ten years.
2. The employment needs having been thus estimated, calculate the number of workers that will have to be replaced because of accidental deaths and retirements. This means that the average age of workers in the industry must be known as well as the rate of retirement.
3. From the estimated total number of workers to be employed during the next ten years, calculate likely employment in the individual industries under the assumptions (a) that the past trend in the ratio of employment in the industry to the total industrial employment (*i.e.,* relative growth or decline) will continue; or if conditions indicate it, (b) that the industry has become purely cyclical (*i.e.,* employment will be proportional to changes in general industrial employment without any trend.)

An accumulation of studies of such current employment trends and a recognition of worker-uniqueness as well as worker-likenesses have led to the conclusion on the part of many educators and counselors that traditional courses of study must be revised to meet new needs. The end is individual growth through the individual's own challenged effort. Curricular changes are made only because of the belief that by them greater individual student effort, not less, can be challenged.

**Stimulation of Economic Thinking**

Since we desire to formulate curricula which will prepare young people for life as they are going to find it, a sensible approach is to determine what in our American scene has contributed in large measure to our present standard of living, and then to prepare curricula which will aid youth to contribute to the betterment of that standard. The president of the Massachusetts Institute of Technology, Dr. Karl Compton, taking the long look, holds that: "The only way more people can buy more is for more people to produce more. The only way we can produce more is to improve our process of production and produce more efficiently. The *next* question is distribution. It is rather clear ; that the gains that come from more efficient production must be passed along three ways: to the consumer in lower prices, to the worker in higher wages, to the investors in more profits."

*Production* is, then, our golden key and *distribution* is the using of that key to unlock the possibilities of better living for more people. One end of today's curricula is to prepare students to produce and to distribute effectively in whatever work area they are, be it research, medicine, or shoelaces. Industry and business will furnish many of the channels for greater production and distribution. It may be that from industry educators can gain a helpful hint for the formulation of curricula which will enable students to have a part in greater production and distribution.

Mr. Clarence Francis, president of the General Foods Corporation, issues the challenging statement that brambles have grown up in our "good American backyard" where the weeds of doubt, fear, discouragement, and "isms" have been allowed to get a roothold. What is needed by American students is a public-school curriculum which is saturated with American principles. In the words of General Hugh H. Johnson, the former Administrator of the National Industrial Recovery Act. The thing that built this country and made these opportunities by the million was private initiative. We want government to curb private abuses but allow the dynamic force of 130,000,000 people to go ahead with the least possible restrictions to produce the results we all long for.

The type of emphasis which leaders of industry feel will most aid young people is pointed out by Mr. Alfred P. Sloan, Jr., Chairman of the board of directors of the General Motors Corporation:

... I want to say most earnestly to you young men that the only sound solution of the problems of a higher standard of living, of reduced unemployment, of expansion of business, in fact, your opportunity in the future from the industrial stand point, is aggressive capitalisation of technological progress, in creasing the productivity of the worker, enabling industry to pay higher wages and reducing the prices of goods and services so that they may be brought within the reach of an ever-increasing number. It is the only way.

Fundamentally there are just two approaches to accomplish everything that all desire to accomplish, providing more things for more people in more places. They are increased efficiency, through the capitalisation of technological improvement, and more work. There lies the answer and the only solution.

Dr. Charles F. Roos, president of The Institute of Applied Econometrics, summarizes for the educator some of the fundamental principles which these industrialists have emphasised and which are basic to our economy:

... the durable goods problem ... is the outstanding problem of our twentieth century economy. An abundance or durable goods characterizes a high-level economy and with durable goods go instability and wide cyclical swings. The appalling complexities posed by this characteristic feature of a high level economy have even induced some persons to give it up entirely and recommend a return to the simple life of an economy centered mainly on the production of perishable goods, controlled (i.e., impeded) production, or a moratorium on invention. Industry's hint to today's curriculum formulators would seem to be that industry will welcome most eagerly chose young people who present themselves to it positively prepared in attitudes, vision, and training to produce and distribute in accordance with the American principles of private initiative.

**Individualisation of Curricula**

Significantly it is worth to note here that a curriculum which meets the needs of the individual student in today's economic order does not aim to make school life easy. Life after school isn't easy. Life in school is just as real an experience in living as is life out of it. The student, the teacher, and the guidance worker must realize that any modification of the curriculum is made only because the individual student's capacities are such that by taking full advantage of that modification he can produce more effective results—do better, harder, and more work. As Dr. Harold C. Campbell puts it: "By all means, let us seek out individual interests and measure individual abilities, but at the same time let us not lose sight of the fact that throughout life things distasteful and things difficult must be faced manfully."

Any system of guidance which encourages youth to quit rather than to persevere, to turn for help outside himself rather than within himself when confronted with problems, has failed. Any system of guidance has also failed which wastes children's youth, teachers' time, and taxpayers' money in an endeavor to obtain the same type of reactions toward the same type of stimuli from *different individuals.*

Much is being written and said and thought about the falling birth rate and the supposed subsequent lessened demand for teachers. An educational approach which would educate the individual child in terms of his unique capacities would soon utilize many more trained educators than are now in the field. The process of continuously challenging the pupil with something which he can do, but for which he needs every whit of his capacity and power, is not to soften anybody—neither the teacher, who must sufficiently understand the child and the subject to provide such a programme, nor the child who adopts the programme, nor the society which must absorb the child who has learned to function effectively with whatever powers are his. In our present public-school curricula the upper group soon become bored with the school programme, which is geared for the average, because they have got in the first ten minutes of the class period what the average child is using thirty minutes to get. Hence, for twenty minutes the brilliant child is learning the "Fine Art of being bored, without seeming to be so," if his behavior report is to be satisfactory. The under-average child is probably spending the best part of thirty minutes being bored because the presentation which is given for the "average" group is too involved and too difficult for him to follow with interest. Research during the past twenty years has shown so definitely that something must be done to fit the programme to the degree of intelligence of the receiving mind, that much trial-and-error experimentation is now under way in an attempt to further the solution of this problem.

The counselor's part in any school situation is to push any programme which will educate more completely each individual child. It is highly probable that education will not find its highest form in any one kind of group education alone, but instead, perhaps, in an intelligent combination of the old tutorial system plus progressive group methods.

**Educational Attitude, Intelligence and the Curriculum**

For the counselor and the student *educational* aptitudes as related to degrees and kinds of intelligence and the curriculum are of equal importance. What are the subjects in the curriculum of the school which most nearly fit the student for those occupational areas in which his life seemingly can be most effective? What changes should be made in the curriculum to make it more adequately fit the needs of students who are being trained for an economic order which is in flux? Finally, what shall be done for the students in the various intelligence ranges so far as pure academic curricula are concerned?

It should be remembered that the counselor must be familiar with the purpose and range of the educational programme of his school if he is to interpret the school to the pupils. In the recent Inquiry into the Character and Cost of Education in the Schools of New York State, conducted by a Committee of the Regents of the State, the goal of secondary education was set as "social competency." In the Report of the Inquiry, we find the following statement, which is of significance in I its bearing upon a guidance program:

> No matter how rich its curricular and extracurricular programme may be, a school cannot do all it should for its pupils unless it sees that each boy and girl gets from its programme the kind of teaching that he especially needs. This means that the school has a number of responsibilities beyond the mere offering of courses. The school ought to know what the individual needs of its pupils are. It ought to make its teaching flexible enough so that boys and girls studying the same subjects may profit from them just as fully as their individual capacities and interests allow. It ought to assure itself that each pupil selects the particular subject most likely to be of benefit to him. It ought to see that when a pupil leaves school he gives himself a fair chance to make use of what his school work has taught him. Failing provision for any of these matters, the school programme is bound to be only partially effective.

Life during and after school hours daily, and after one has completed or quit school, is a continuum; social competence after school is often predicated by educational competence in school, and educational competence is largely determined by proper curricula. Guidance is concerned with the child as he is in his total environment, which in school includes and emphasizes his educational programme. It is just as necessary that his educational programme be selected in terms of his potentialities as it is that his other major plans be set in accordance with them. It is, therefore, a major concern of guidance to place the child, as far as practicable, in that part of the school system and in the particular curriculum which is designed to develop his potential trends with the highest degree of knowledge and skill that it is possible for him to achieve. Then, as a follow-up on such educational guidance, it is the counselor's duty to direct the child's attention to those areas of economic life where the knowledge and skill acquired will find an outlet.

The same tools are necessary for educational counselling that are used in all other types of counselling. However, the "cumulative record" is of special importance for educational guidance, for it is in part a definite record of past educational performance. A second area of knowledge which is indispensable to the educational counselor is knowledge of the spread and scope of local and available secondary education; together with the objectives of each school and course, the counselor must know, as far as it; is now possible to know, which types of schools and which individual courses within these schools provide the best preparatory background for those functional occupational areas for which the individual evidences the greatest in-herent potential trends. This is a large order. Much research must be completed and evaluated before this procedure can cease to be the ideal of educational guidance and become its reality

Currently only the dim outlines for such educational

guidance are known. For example, if a student's I.Q. is above 115, it can be safely suggested to him that an academic college course is advisable. If *it* is less than 115, there are many factors to be considered before college is advised: (1) What are his most outstanding ability trends? (2) Is college an asset in a life occupation which utilizes these ability trends? (3) Will the student develop into a stronger individual if he utilizes his four years in his life occupation with an avocational interest only in the cultural side of life? (4) Considering the fairly limited meaning of college training for the student whose I.Q. is under 115, is college economically worth the sacrifice which would, perhaps, be entailed by the youth and his family? (5) is there a possibility that the continued experience of academic mediocrity may set for the individual the habit of mediocrity in his achievement and, thus when he does enter the functional occupational areas where his abilities should win success for him, will he be content even there with a mediocre performance?

The rating of 115 or less has been arbitrarily selected. The same thoughts could equally well have been written about 112 or less. We refer to the general borderline group between average and high-average abstract intelligence for the total population—that group which is found approximately between 110 I.Q. and 115 I.Q.

The joy and reward and triumph of educational counselling comes when a student whose I.Q. is 130 or above *is* the educational counselor. For these students the counselor must remove mountains. The future of progress depends their leadership. It is not only recognised but emphasised that much more than a high I.Q. is needed for creative progress, but the high I.Q. is an essential ingredient, and it is rare. An I.Q. of above 130 is a continuing challenge to the guidance worker never to let go until the student is well on his way toward an optimum achievement of his potentialities. In the experiences of the authors, there has been no student with an I.Q. of 130 or more for whom a college education was not a distinct advantage which should be sought and obtained regardless of the barriers which had to be overcome in order to obtain it.

For the students whose I.Q. is 95 or under, college is definitely not recommended. For all students certain occupational-ability trends will be more outstanding than others. Those students of the mental order below 95 I.Q. should, through adequate educational guidance while in high school, be given that subject background which seems most helpful for the functional occupational area in which their capacity trends place them.

Realizing that in the face of inadequate and incomplete research the job of educational guidance is being, and must be, done, we suggest here that in the interest of furthering guidance knowledge, each guidance counselor should work; out some very simple organisation for his counselor recommendations and findings, and year by year note the results obtained and, as new facts are learned, report them. It is suggested that short case histories be given for individuals in each of the following categories:

1. *I.Q. 130 and above:* Extra-heavy high-school academic course recommended, then college, and then a life of some type of creative endeavor or analytical or professional work.

2. I.Q. *115 to 130:* Academic course recommended; also college, with a suggested development along certain broad functional professional lines. For example, to an individual whose I.Q. was 120, whose social intelligence was 140, whose class popularity had caused him to hold school offices throughout his public-school career, whose mechanical aptitude was low, and for whom science and mathematics were the curriculum's most difficult subjects, it was suggested by one of the authors that in college he consider preparing

himself for a profession success in which definitely required the ability to get along with people. There are many occupations and professions in which the main task is to understand one's fellow man and to make him like and understand you. This boy majored in advertising in college and is now doing effective work as a state legislator. For the individuals in this group little more than a planned and intelligent suggestion need be given.

Probably one of the most effective means of guidance in this group is to think through the problem with the counselor as was done in the case just given, for each case is unique. It was suggested to a boy with the same I.Q. but with a social-intelligence score of 100, and with a great interest in mathematics and high manual dexterity, that he consider sonic phase of engineering. Accordingly, he went to a leading institute of technology, and today is a successful mechanical engineer.

3. *For I.Q. under 115*: For persons with an I.Q. under 110 it is suggested that the case is exceptional in which a college education is worth the time spent on it. Among those individuals between 95 and 115 in I.Q. who have no imperative reason for going to college, all who show a high mechanical aptitude might well be guided to trade schools. For those in this I.Q. range whose social intelligence is high but whose mechanical aptitude is low, the distributive occupations are suggested. Since knowledge of the articles to be distributed and effective methods of distribution are essential here, it is suggested that where such Courses do not exist, the counselor's part is to call attention to the need for them and to do everything possible to see to it that such courses are provided.

4. For the one-talent individual whose I.Q. is below 95, that one talent will determine the counselor's suggestions. After having determined the one talent and having suggested the type of school and the course which will most aid

in its development, the next most important help the counselor can give to the counselor is to awaken a wholesome attitude toward the "one-talent job." If janitor work is to be his, the social usefulness of cleanliness can be so stressed, and truthfully so, that a sense of dignity will go with the individual as he attempts to be a good janitor. "It's not what you do but how well you do it that counts" is the burden of the suggestions which it is well to give to those of this low I.Q. group. However, even here there are special abilities—high manual dexterity, and a keen eye, and a general sense of order and neatness—which lead to those phases of functional endeavor which have to do with cleaning. A phlegmatic individual with a high index-finger reaction time might well be trained for those factory operations which require the work of an automaton. This individual will be happy in such a job; it is his right, whereas it is criminal to put a 130-I.Q. individual there unless the management wants to know how to make some type of mechanical improvement.

What has been given here, and what is now known by workers everywhere in the field of guidance, is admittedly only a beginning. The cry of every counselor must be, "Light, more light!" and if, at the end of a year of counselling, a counselor feels that there has been no new finding, no fresh bit of guidance knowledge acquired, that counselor would do well to ponder long the measure of his own success as a counselor.

**School and Brilliant Student**

The student whose intelligence score is in the very high ratings carries within himself the lamp by which the way of progress is lighted. For the benefit of all humankind these individuals who have the ability to pioneer the way to better things must be given every opportunity and every encouragement. During the secondary-school period it is the counselor's part to see to it that these students *are* given a thorough training in the broad fundamentals of a college preparatory course together with much of character building and club and play activities. These individuals are the '"queen" bees of the hive. "To him that hath it shall be given" must be made to come true for them, every one, if they are to give to society the gift which is theirs to give. It is the counselor's task to see to it that those things for which these individuals have need are theirs. It is essential that these students have all that the accumulated wisdom of the ages can give them, so far as that wisdom is related to the area in which their life's contribution will be made. They should receive, therefore, a thorough preparation for college and the experience of college.

**Wrong Job and Brilliant Student**

The thinkers at the genius level form less than one-half of one per cent of the entire population. Yet often these individuals with high native endowments are allowed to leave school, sometimes at a very early age and for purposes of functioning in an occupational area in which high ability is a greater liability than asset; and for these individuals and for society much is lost.

The counselor reaps the largest dividends in his profession when he finds and guides a talented individual.

Examples of one man's brains putting others to work are numerous in industry. One of the authors was a consulting psychologist for a large advertising firm. A young man was considered a problem case and accordingly was, on the lay-off list. He was found to have an Army Alpha rating of 106. His boss had a rating of 90. Two of his previous bosses in the plant had Army Alpha scores of approximately 100. The young man was considered a problem because he was dissatisfied with existing methods. Later adoption of the changes which he recommended saved the company 2 per cent on its gross outlay, and inasmuch as the changes involved an entirely new and more extensive type of darkroom equipment, four permanent additional workers were hired. The young man was placed in a position where his capacities were used, and instead of being laid off, his salary was doubled.

One of the chief aims of the counselor is to see to it that girls and boys of high capacities do receive adequate academic training. Academic training provides the most adequate tools now available for minds which function on the creative levels. If the people who are thus highly endowed can be adequately trained, it is probable that jobs will be available for all who want them, governments and economic cycles notwithstanding. Until this thesis is tried, it cannot be positively stated. Today, industry is so entirely job-centered that its only question is, "Can the man do the job?"—not "What will the job do to the man?" Nor does society concern itself for the lost abilities and the at-tendant unhappiness of the talented individual in the small job. *Nor are such considerations in the immediate province of industry.* Industry's first job is to produce and distribute a product. Education's first task is to guide. *The guidance counselor is in a position of fundamental importance to the happiness and economic security of youth* in the school of today.

Given the native creative power, and given the tools with which to use it, that power can no more be kept from functioning than the tides can be harnessed. Creative power as the highest functioning mental level is not described in terms of I.Q. alone. The I.Q. is but the signal—the red flag which says, "Examine here." The counselor is wise who makes of first importance the counselling of the child whose I.Q. is above 130. After the needs of this group have been met, the remaining time may be given to the other important duties of counselling.

While for the ordinary run-of-the-mill college groups

the same educational and extracurricular counsel as that suggested for the genius group is indicated, with this difference: If some of these individuals are financially unable to attend college, they can probably function just as effectively without college training, provided they are guided toward those occupational areas which challenge their abilities. The legend of the college education has, perhaps, taken too firm a hold on much of modern thought. Many individuals in this run-of-the-mill college intellectual group (approximately no to 130 I.Q.) can gain a four-year start on a fellow-worker who has gone to college, if a challenging and proper occupational area has been chosen, and if the individual has spent his extra energy in satisfying cultural pursuits and in learning the facts which are pertinent to the occupation in which he is engaged. The individual, the occupation, and the economic opportunity necessarily will be determining guidance factors and hence will suggest curricula for this group.

**Below-Average Ability Student**

To every student who will not go to college, our schools owe a debt which, in our opinion, is not being paid. If in democracy we have a system of government worthy of a high-school boy's blood, perhaps to be spilled a few years hence on a battlefield, then certainly that system is worthy of his study while he is yet in school. If the fundamental tenets of our government and our national system are worth living by, they are worth knowing. Before a student leaves school, is it asking too much that he know the Constitution as well as he knows the vagaries of Communism; that he know the favorable position of workingmen in India as compared with that of the workers of any other nation on earth; that he recognize that wealth for the worker or the employer is created only when there is adequate *production* and *distribution;* that the Indian system is not based on *any* X versus *any* Y, but is based on *every* X co-operating with *every* Y for greater production? Haves and have-nots, capital and labor, Jew and Christian, Catholic and non-Catholic, white and black, and all other such ism-producing concepts led to the founding of this land which was to be forever free from them. If there are those who would bring these attitudes to our shores, is it not for our democratic system, through its schools, to create its own attitudes and to teach its own way? The products of Indian system are far from perfect, but they have nothing to fear from comparison with the products of any other existing or non-existing form of government. It is the right of these "almost men and women" who are leaving our schools *to know the facts* —to know that only active participation in our government by every citizen will preserve its best features and keep it strong. On these facts they can build perhaps a greater India. *With these facts given objectively in our schools they will build on an American foundation and in the Indian way.* Without these facts, the half-truths of the "isms" will have no factual standards by which to be measured, and the half-truths of the "isms" may thus seem to be whole truths, and twenty years from now we, the educators of today, may wonder how a superstructure of "isms" came to be erected on the firm foundations of Indian system.

We urge that every student, if possible, beginning as early as the fourth grade, be given facts-scientific, live, objective facts about our economic system and our way of government and, concurrently, just as accurate facts about other economic systems and forms of government. Those students who will either go to college or create for themselves a cultural environment because of their own mental richness will probably have other opportunities to obtain facts. For the below-average child these school years very probably represent a "last chance."

Also, for each major occupational area, for those who are in the below-average group leaving school and who evidence special aptitude for a given area, a cultural course is suggested which emphasizes the history and the romance of that occupational area. Emphasis should be placed upon the major inventions therein and the creative contributions therefrom. Further, the lives of those individuals who have contributed most in these given areas should be studied. Such a course would feed the imaginations of the students whose lives were going to be lived even within a limited sector of an area so presented.

**Conclusion**

The need for a curriculum which stimulates the individual student to function at his optimum both in school and out of it is felt by teachers and counselors and industrialists. For those who believe our system to be worth preserving, a practical approach which emphasizes economic and political thinking based on facts is suggested. That a brilliant mind sparkles and gives light only when confronted with sufficiently difficult tasks to evoke a spark; that the "run-of-the-mill mind" gasps for air and sinks in despair when given too difficult tasks, and wallows in laziness when given tasks too simple; and that the below-average mind functions best when stimulated not too much, is recognised by those who are formulating the curricula for today's schools.

# 3

# Guidance in Schools

"Although this may seem a paradox, all exact science is dominated by the idea of approximation. When a man tells you, that he knows the exact truth about anything, you are safe in inferring that he is an inexact man."

—*Bertrand Russell*

Vocational guidance, is generally associated today with the duties of a member of the school staff called a careers teacher, but it is difficult to speak in precise terms about the nature of this appointment. H.R. King (1953) suggested that the origins of the office lay in the traditional role of the headmaster, or in a boarding school, of the housemaster, as leaders of a community traditionally committed to the welfare of its members. Hence one might have hoped that careers guidance would develop as part of a broader concept of guidance. Unfortunately this did not happen. The Headmasters' Employment Committee set up in 1918 was concerned with the narrower problems of advising older school-leavers about employment and placement. This was the approach followed where careers services slowly spread out through secondary schools during the next two decades.

Even with such restricted goals, the services do not seem to have been very effective, as King admits from pre-war research studies in London. There is still no overall agreement among educationists about basic principles of guidance work, and there is no law which compels a school to offer careers guidance as a subject, either within the curriculum or outside it. In this situation one would expect to find piecemeal development, with individual programmes devised and controlled by the staff of individual schools. Wide differences of opinion might be expected to develop between schools about the aims of guidance, about its methods, about the amount of curricular time necessary for it, and about the qualifications necessary in the member of staff responsible for directing a guidance programme. As provision is not compulsory, many schools might be expected to have no formal programme, and perhaps no careers teacher as such.

Since the war, research in Britain has indeed suggested that the provision of vocational guidance is in an unsatisfactory state. Michael Carter made a detailed investigation of guidance influences on 100 boys and 100 girls in 1959, drawn at random from the Sheffield area, by means of three interviews held with them during the period of their transition from school to work. The results indicated that these young people had received little effective guidance throughout their school years; most of them had only a very hazy idea about what their teachers had, said on the subject; parents often took little interest in the school; jobs were often chosen without any real thought, and the schools had not integrated the work of the Youth Employment Officers in any satisfactory manner. In 1964 the Careers Research Advisory Centre (CRAC) carried out studies of the position of vocational guidance in 224 British schools, and found that just under half of these had no careers teacher at all. In the same year, the National Union of Teachers carried out a survey based on over a hundred questionnaires returned from a sample of careers teachers in English schools. These showed that careers facilities, such as a careers room, were often lacking for these staff; about half of them said that they did all their work in their spare time; and where careers work was allocated a place on the timetable it usually amounted to no more than four periods a week (a period may vary in length from about half an hour to an hour).

K.R. Alien carried out a survey of 2,024 young men in Liverpool most of whom had been apprentices in 1961, about the careers advice they had received on leaving school. His results suggested that under 10% of those coming from grammar and secondary modern schools had found their first job mainly through the help of the school, although this rose to just over 21% for those from technical schools. Between 38% and 45% of the adolescents had relied on their families for help. The Schools Council Enquiry based on national samples from maintained secondary schools in England and Wales in 1968, found that among young school leavers aged 15, 63% of boys and 48% of girls found jobs through parents, relatives and friends. During the winter of 1965-66, a group of twelve students from a Lancashire college of education made over seventy visits to youth clubs in and around Liverpool, to interview groups of school children and young leavers about the guidance they had received in school. In every case over half the club members said they had received no guidance in school, or could remember such advice only in the most hazy way. The poverty of careers advice at schools has also been remarked by industrial training officers in Britain, such as W. Parker (1966).

There is some evidence that this picture is changing rather rapidly. The Schools Council Enquiry (1968) surveyed the provision of careers teachers in 111 secondary maintained schools in England and Wales from which children often left at age 15. They found that 87% had one or more teachers who looked after careers work as part of their job. But they also found that in over half the schools these careers teachers had no training for their work at all, and only 4% of the schools contained teachers with more than a fortnight's training.

First of all, there seems to be a residue of ignorance in our schools about the importance of vocational guidance, and of its wider implications. This is pointed out by the earlier surveys, which suggested that until recently the actual provision of careers teachers in schools was scanty. Even though the Schools Council Enquiry of 1968 suggests that this is changing, it also indicates an alarming lack of adequately trained teachers for the work. The blindness of many school heads to the real problems of vocational guidance is highlighted by further evidence from the 1968 Schools Council Enquiry: 49% of school principals felt that enough was already being done to prepare pupils for life after school, and 58% felt that careers advice was sufficient already.

There is a brighter side to this picture. As the evidence suggests, an expansion of interest in careers guidance seems to be starting in the schools. Even though training in vocational guidance is still rare in colleges of education and in post-graduate diploma courses in education, a start has been made in a few places; and during the last decade the Institutes of Education of Reading, Keele, and Exeter, have developed advanced diploma courses in guidance theory and practice. A similar course at Swansea is in preparation. London University Institute of Education started an advanced diploma course in Adolescent Development in 1968, which, while not aiming to train guidance specialists as such, emphasizes the importance of the problems.

Because there is so much variation in the pattern of guidance arrangements in British schools, a detailed description of the different approaches becomes impracticable; and one cannot describe any one programme as 'typical'. In this chapter we shall consider some of the problems which occur in designing and running guidance work in schools, and at some of the solutions which are being attempted.

## In-Charge of the Guidance Programme

*(a) School Principal*

On the surface, there seems to be every reason to locate guidance in the hands of the school head; he is usually one of the most experienced teachers in the school, and the one to whom parents mainly come to discuss their children's problems. A subject approved and directed by the principal himself is lifted out of the general run of extra-curricular jobs and accorded a higher status; provision of curricular time for it becomes easier; and it would be reasonable for a guidance team, if later formed, to be led by the head teacher. Finally, such a person might to some extent bridge the gap between educational and vocational guidance, since he has the authority to follow a pupil's career right through school, and to guide him both in his choice of courses and in his choice of work.

There are a number of arguments against this arrangement. Under a bureaucratic system the modern head teacher tends to become an administrator, the more so as school sizes grow. It does not follow that the qualities of a successful administrator are those of a successful counselor; there may even be some conflict of roles between today's ideal school principal and that of a guidance specialist for pupils. Again, how is a head teacher, who meets many calls on his time, to fit in such duties as home visiting, liaison with firms and industries, and discussion with other guidance specialists? Is he likely to find much time for individual pupil guidance? While his value in according recognition, status and administrative support for careers work can hardly be questioned, it might be better to delegate the details of guidance to members of a supporting team, or perhaps even better, to let them divide the duties among themselves. The practicality of such a policy for larger secondary schools has been accepted in the Seebohm Report in 1968. Occasionally however, school principals refuse to delegate certain functions—such as liaison with parents—which they identify with their own work. The final outcome of such an attitude will depend on the extent to which the principal is able—and willing—to undertake the work himself.

*(b) Careers Teacher*

An arrangement whereby vocational guidance is in the hands of a single member of staff who takes the job on largely as an extra-curricular activity has little to commend it; and the disadvantages of this form of organisation increase with the size of the school. Such a person must very often depend upon secondhand data about the classroom achievement of pupils; unless he is given much free time he cannot personally keep in touch with many parents, or make adequate contact with the world of work. For similar reasons his liaison with other guidance specialists such as the Youth Employment Officer, the school psychologist and the school medical officer, is necessarily limited. If in addition he has only four periods a week of curricular time for his work, there is no effective way of solving these problems. Here the teacher may have to offer a service rather different, aimed at providing as much careers information as possible to senior pupils, and hoping for the best. Perhaps this is why the careers programmes of many schools seem to contain little more than an information service. In these circumstances it is quite natural that careers work should be regarded as nothing more important than any other extra-curricular activity, which, along with the running of the chess club and the jazz society, may in a few unfortunate schools be farmed out to whatever teacher happens to be available. Where guidance at different levels is necessary, as in comprehensive schools, the services of a number of staff become essential, and pupils may in practice turn for advice to individual teachers where the careers teacher cannot provide an adequate service.

*(c) Form and House Teachers*

The argument for placing guidance exclusively in the hands of teachers holding these positions is that they are anyway responsible for giving advice on personal and educational matters to pupils as a consequence of their position. They are thus likely to have close knowledge of their charges, and so to have prepared the ground for further guidance functions. Knowledge of even a few schools shows the error of such argument, as the terms 'form teacher' and 'house master' can be applied in an arbitrary way to many different sorts of position: a form master may have close knowledge of his pupils, or he may be responsible only for administrative functions such as checking attendance and collating end-of-year examination marks. Likewise the term 'house master' may denote a variety of valuable guidance functions, or it might be purely nominal. Differences in the terms of their appointments, the nature of their contacts with children, the length of time they stay in the job, and their private attitudes to guidance, will all qualify the value of the guidance they offer. Generalisations about who should organize such work, which offer easy solutions by assuming that a standard system of appointments exists already in the schools, should be avoided.

*(d) Specially Trained Teacher*

The teacher trained in techniques of guidance through a specialist course can be expected to provide more adequate guidance than the untrained. Two factors are largely responsible for this. Specific courses in guidance are at present operating only in Reading, Exeter and Keele universities, all of which are comparatively new in the field, and each year turn out fewer than thirty students apiece. This is not enough to alter the national provision significantly. Moreover, in general, teachers must be prepared to break their careers to take these courses, and secondment from employment is not always granted. Second, graduates in psychology with post-graduate training and teaching experience, who could supply the necessary specialist knowledge, are not often found on the school staff. Graduates with this background are very much in demand in the field of educational psychology, where their salaries are generally higher than they could get with the same qualifications and experience in classroom teaching. Hutchinson and Young (1962) have produced a set of graphs which vividly illustrate how unfavourably teachers' salaries compare with those of, other professions, and until this injustice is redressed, schools are likely to remain short of graduate guidance specialists.

*(e) Guidance Team of School Staff*

In spite of what we have just said, there may be good reasons for using existing school staff as members of a guidance team.

Our first case is a nine-stream comprehensive school situated on a post-war housing estate in north Bristol, and drawing its enrolment of over 1,500 children from the estate and adjacent areas. A full time staff of over seventy teachers is employed. Guidance is effected by combining the efforts of different teams in support of a central careers team, whose composition will be described later. On entry the children spend two years under a form system in the lower school. Academic guidance is the responsibility of the subject teachers, but pastoral care is handled by nine form teachers, all under the general authority of the head of the lower school. In the third year pupils are divided amongst six houses for all non-teaching activities, and within the house their interests are looked after by house tutors, responsible to the careers team, and working with them, under the head of the middle school. There are approximately 140 children in each house.

In the sixth form, which has over 150 students, the form master and specialist tutors combine with the careers staff and with subject tutors. Continuity of records is maintained by subject heads, housemasters and house tutors. This complex arrangement is set out in diagrammatic form. The careers team itself is composed as follows: (a) The careers master. He is responsible for boys and girls leaving from the fifth year (CSE and O level G.C.E.), and those leaving from the sixth years who are not seeking full time education later. (b) The careers mistress. She is responsible for boys and girls leaving from the fourth year, lower fifth, and girls leaving from the fifth and sixth year commercial course. (c) The last member of this team, the sixth form master, concerns himself solely with the problems of university, technical college and college of education entry.

Team work in this school is part of a carefully organised guidance system. Members of staff who belong to these teams are paid an additional allowance for the work. Its importance is a so suggested by the provision of a capitation allowance for the careers department to cover the costs of stationery and printing; the arrangement of a careers room with a telephone and extensive filing cabinet space, adjacent to a careers library, as well as individual offices for the careers master and mistress. In addition the careers staff are given about twice as much free time as normal staff, to allow them to prepare programmes, and a small amount of curricular time is provided for teaching courses in careers work as well. As a result, close liaison can be maintained with the Youth Employment officer and with the outside world of work.

Our second case comes from a technical high school in the midlands of England. With an enrolment of just over 800 boys and girls, the school is bilateral with intake partly based on the results of the Local Education Authority's 11+ examination. For the first three years the pupils follow a common curriculum. During the third year they undergo an assessment course which is unusually elaborate, involving tests of ability, aptitudes, interests, as well as academic attainment. After interview with the pupils and consultation with parents, pupils then join one of four streams, academic, scientific, technical or commercial. The school is organised on a house basis and on year units, each of which has a tutor-in-charge within the house. House masters are responsible for following the progress of each individual child, and for keeping record cards. In their fourth and fifth years, pupils see their house tutors once a week, when careers are discussed. It is appreciated however that house masters cannot know about every career, and certain members of staff are therefore appointed as careers advisers: The head of the engineering department advises on engineering courses, and likewise the heads of the commerce and science courses on their respective careers. The head of the biology department advises on nursing and allied careers, the deputy head on entry to universities and polytechnics and the senior mistress on entry to colleges of education. Each of these specialists also maintains contact with developments in his or her own area, both at notional and local level, and is responsible for the provision of new information. To coordinate this, a further member of staff acts as careers administration officer, and arranges for the distribution and filing of the relevant information. Finally the Youth Employment Officer is brought into the vocational guidance work at a number of stages, and is another member of the team.

Although this school has a less involved guidance system than the first example, both schools show careful organisation, the division of responsibility between different members of stiff, and the recognition that effective guidance cannot be carried out by one person alone. Common also to both schools is the provision of a special member of staff to deal with the problems of entry to higher education. Because of the great pressures now exerted on the institutions available for this, in particular the universities, great care must be taken in choosing colleges which are likely to accept the applicant. It is by no means uncommon to find students in colleges of education who have all the qualifications for a university, but have been unfortunate in those to which they applied. Apart from this, the appearance of new institutions, other than universities, which teach, for degrees (such as polytechnics) have made guidance in this field more complex than ever.

A guidance team may also include people other than the school staff, as the third case indicates. This is a grammar school near Manchester, where vocational guidance is handled by two careers masters, the local Youth Employment Officer, and Careers Advisory Officers, the last two being enlisted from outside the school. The division of work is as follows:

1. Pupils at the end of their third year decide what subjects to take in their forthcoming G.C.E. O level examinations. The careers teacher emphasize; the importance attached by universities and other institutions of higher education, and professional bodies, to gaining passes in certain subjects, such as English and Mathematics.
2. At the beginning of their fifth year, County Careers Advisory Service pamphlets are issued to each pupil, and in October, Careers Advisory Officers give general talks to the year group on how to approach a career choice.
3. In the spring term of the fifth year each pupil is interviewed individually by a group consisting of a Careers Advisory Officer, the local Youth Employment Officer, and one of the careers masters, who has previously discussed the pupil with members of staff who teach him. These interviews are frequently inconclusive, and are followed up a few weeks later by further interviews with one of the careers teachers.
4. Throughout the remainder of the year, a careers teacher

acts as middleman between leavers and the Youth Employment Officer, keeping each leaver's employment situation under review.

5. In the sixth form, a careers teacher advises on entry to higher education and other work. Where the problems of any pupil appear to require professional advice, the Careers Advisory Officer is again called in.

In advising on the careers value of school subjects, the careers master here is recognising the relationship between educational and vocational guidance. Some guidance problems cannot be handled within the school and need expert advice by the Careers Advisory Officer. The question of what experts outside the school should ideally be used in team guidance, and in what way, is dealt with more fully in a later chapter. Space does not permit of more than these detailed examples. Many other sorts of team organisation exist. For instance: in a grammar school, the principal as guidance specialist, supported by the deputy principal and a careers mistress (the latter handling details of day to day work); the school principal giving general advice, with sixth form tutors giving specialist advice; a careers master working alone, but with authority to recruit other staff from time to time, as needed (a poor concept of team work); and guidance divided between the school principal and a part-time careers teacher, employed solely for this work.

**Starting Vocational Guidance**

Vocational guidance during the last year or sometimes even the last term of school life, may be described as *crisis counselling,* a term also used to describe any last minute attempt at guidance. Its disadvantages are that by this time the student has already committed himself to certain courses which cannot easily be changed; and in crisis counselling no amount of testing can show the dynamic pattern of development which continuous guidance charts.

Sometimes careers teachers argue that short, concentrated periods of advice to pupils just before they leave are the best solution in the present circumstances, where little time is allowed for organising a complex guidance scheme. But complexity is not reduced by this, if all leavers are to be given a fairly equal treatment. The exception of secondary modem, maintained, and all-age schools, leavers are in general spread out across every age range from fifteen to nineteen years. In the case of comprehensive, technical and grammar schools, crisis counselling would require many periodic bursts of advice to leavers. Moreover the nature of the advice would have to be geared to the different needs of groups leaving at different ages. It would also be difficult to integrate the work of the Youth Employment Officer and other specialists under such conditions. The fact that in secondary modern schools most pupils leave between the ages of fifteen and sixteen may encourage careers staff to concentrate on short course planning. But in any case pupils leave these schools from every term of the final year, as they reach the legal school leaving age, and so at least three courses would have to be provided each year, cutting the time for any one course to less than a term. Apart from other objections then, crisis counselling appears clumsy even as a makeshift solution. Guidance seen as a continuous process starting from the date of entry by pupils to secondary education appears to offer these advantages:

(i) Although objective psychometric tests only give a static picture of the individual at a moment in time, a programme of continuous guidance ,males it possible to use batteries of tests at different times, so allowing staff to trace the pattern of change.

(ii) The development of the individual can be observed, and perhaps related to some general theory such as that of Super, mentioned earlier in this book.

(iii) When educational and vocational guidance are seen

as part of the same process, there is more hope that the subjects studied in secondary school will have some bearing on the work taken up after the pupil leaves.

(iv) The child may develop a more responsible attitude to his own future where this is made an important study in its own right throughout school.

(v) In a lengthy guidance scheme, a greater overall amount of careers information can be passed on to the pupil.

(vi) Many important aspects of guidance can be covered before the earliest pupils begin to leave.

Even if we accept that educational, vocational and personal guidance are three aspects of the same thing, the range of problems to be covered is likely to vary from school to school. Vocational guidance can broadly concentrate on the problems of leaving over a narrow age range from fifteen to sixteen years old; on the other hand the graphs suggest that under 10% of grammar school pupils leave at age fifteen, and there are peaks of leaving at ages sixteen and eighteen respectively, suggesting that leaving is related to the outcome of the G.C.E. examinations at O and A levels. Comprehensive, technical, multi-and bilateral schools present the greatest problems, as they produce large numbers of early and late leavers. Any school will from time to time throw up very diverse problems of guidance among its pupils; but in planning courses, staff might find that by studying the pattern of leaving from their own school over a period of years an initial answer to the question of range might be given.

As the Schools Council Enquiry on Young Leavers (1968) has indicated, early leavers often differ from other pupils in terms of social class; they tend to come from homes where physical conditions and resources are not conducive to study, and where there is no tradition of extended learning or any clear understanding of the purposes and methods of today's teaching. They tend to aim for immediate rather than distant goals; they put high value on preparation for work, everyday living, the desire to be grown-up, and practical interests. They tend to show little interest in school, improvement of career prospects, or intellectual-aspirations. Pupils who stay beyond the statutory leaving age tend to come from homes more conducive to study; they identify more closely with the school and accept its discipline; they have higher intellectual and academic aspirations, and are more interested in improving their career prospects.

Most schools maintain some system for recording information about their pupils, such as the date of birth, name and address of parents, name of primary school attended age, height, weight on admittance, and thereafter annually. Progress through secondary school is frequently measured by the comments of form and subject teachers, taken at the end of term or academic year. Participation in school games, appointment to posts of responsibility (such as prefect), and success in external examinations may be entered, as well as notes about what specialist subjects the student has chosen to study. In addition, serious breaches of discipline may be recorded. Much of this is objective information, from which the reader can draw his own conclusions. But in addition, record cards may require their compiler, often a form teacher, to assess the pupil's qualities of persistence, loyalty, adjustment and so on. Such questions call for objective judgment based on a narrow range of observations, and the answers may be misleading. The same is true where the record sheet calls for the teacher to make a general assessment of the pupil's ability and aptitudes. It would be hazardous even for a mental assessment expert to derive the pattern of aptitudes from performance in the limited areas of schoolwork. But the idea that a form teacher can best talk about abilities, progress and aptitudes is still occasionally mooted as a responsible opinion.

Disadvantage of many current forms of school assessment is that they are based on a limited form of comparison. A possible remedy for this would be to use standardised attainment tests wherever possible. The National Foundation for Educational Research publishes such standardised tests in English Progress, Sentence Reading, Vocabulary, Comprehension, Continuous Prose, Mechanical Arithmetic, Arithmetic Progress, Geometry, Algebra and Trigonometry, and their lists are well worth consulting for other tests as well. These span children's ages from seven to sixteen years and are suitable for use in junior as well as secondary schools. They are available to teachers on production of a written authority from the head of the school or institution in which they are serving, and are thus open for general use.

### Frequent Omissions from Present School Records

*(a) Social Background*

Very often only the most scanty information is available to teachers about the social background of their pupils, although as we have already seen in an earlier chapter, there are some grounds for thinking that this may be one of the most important limiting factors on the effective development of patterns of thought, communication, and measured intelligence. These alone are good enough reasons for including on a record the fullest possible data, about home influence. But this can be very difficult to obtain, because of the presence of a communication barrier between lower working class parents and the teaching staff. The presence of such a barrier has been suggested by a number of writers, including Jackson and Maraden (1962). The authors found that whereas middle class parents used the school as a service, and were not frightened to make complaints and put questions to the school staff, lower working class parents worried about this, felt insecure when talking to such people, found difficulty in arranging interviews with those in authority generally, and sometimes rejected the whole idea of contact with middle class people who could have helped to guide their children.

The Schools Council Enquiry on Young Leavers (1968) has suggested that what appears as a lack of interest by working class parents may be the result of three attitudes. These are: (1) the delegation of all responsibility for education to the school, together with a failure to see the need for any contact unless something is wrong; (2) an idea among the parents that they would be interfering if they went to the school uninvited; (3) a lack of confidence in being able to conduct a satisfactory discussion with the teachers if they did go.

If we are to make the most of the opportunities offered by the new wide-scale development of comprehensive secondary education, the problems of identifying and handling home background difficulties must be squarely faced. These difficulties are dealt with in later sections of this book. In the long run, what is needed is a reorganisation of all guidance services, to integrate their efforts, and to speed the location of guidance problems. Two pressing needs at present seem to be: (a) to get information about educational and work opportunities across to parents in lower working classes, and to record the results, or lack of them; and (b) to obtain and record information about home conditions in every case where a child's school performance or behaviour appears to be inadequate. One way, not much used, of supplying the first need, might be for vocational information to be sent regularly to pupils' parents, whether they ask for it or not. Perhaps this could be done in a cumulative way by including it or the end of term report, which might also mention suitable educational courses for the pupil's future. To meet the second need, closer links are clearly needed between school staff and social workers.

*(b) Medical Records*

The school doctor or nurse usually possesses information on the medical background of individual pupils; but this is often kept separate from the pupil's general records. Guidance staff may be given such information at the discretion of the doctor. This is unfortunate, as the absence of such data can greatly reduce the value of any cumulative record. One needs to know the frequency of medical treatment, for what conditions, and in particular about chronic conditions, such as colour blindness, high frequency deafness, the after effects of brain injury, functional nervous disorders, defective speech, and so on, which may affect educational achievement, personal morale, or vocational possibilities. The main reason why medical data are not entered on records is the refusal of doctors to permit what might amount to publication of facts about individual patients. A second reason is that the facts might be misunderstood by lay readers. In psychology, it is a general condition of the sale of tests in this country and the United States that numerical results (such as I.Q., raw and percentile scores on tests of interests, aptitudes, and personality) should not be disclosed to any persons lacking accepted training in their interpretation, which few teachers have in our schools today. Super and Crites (1962), suggest that a possible solution would be for such data to be restated in terms which the layman can understand, and which would not allow him to misinterpret them. Might this not also be possible with medical data?

*(c) Follow-up Information*

Some schools record the first job or course of training taken by leavers. Less usual is a record of job changes during the first years after leaving, difficult to compile without after-school work by guidance staff. The reasons for such changes may vary, from steps along a promotion ladder, to frequent rows with bosses, or personal restlessness. Research done for the Crowther Report indicated that 16% of all secondary school leavers (from secondary modern schools), changed jobs more than three times in the first three years after leaving school. No national figures are available for an overall view, but research in Glasgow, Sheffield, Birmingham and elsewhere suggests that job-changing is quite common among young workers. If it is at all possible then a follow-up study should be earned out to obtain evidence of the value of the guidance given. If a survey of job changes after three years is impracticable, a follow-up might be tried after six months, using a questionnaire to examine the young workers adjustment to his new life. This process will be easiest if the confidence and cooperation of the leavers have been gained while at school, and if they understand the value of filling up the form honestly and returning it. The results of such follow-up procedures should be used to modify the guidance scheme. Without some such feedback of information there can be little insight into the inevitable mistakes and omissions of an early guidance programme.

**Liaison with Outside Agencies**

The main sources of guidance outside school with which guidance staff should be in touch are (a) the parents, (b) the Youth Employment Service, (c) the Child Guidance Services and the School Health Service, (d) the social services concerned with home-visiting, (e) the National Institute of Industrial Psychology, and (f) the Youth Service.

*(a) Liaison with the Working World*

Contact in this area can be used for keeping guidance staff up to date about local employment vacancies; for studying the qualities looked for in applicants by various employers; for keeping a check on the standards of training and promotion offered by local firms; for making firms more aware of the pool of ability present among pupils at the school; for arranging children's visits to local firms, either individually or in groups;

sometimes for attachments of such pupils to firms for a few days at a time; and for arranging the sort of parent-pupil-teacher days, sometimes called careers conventions, described above. At a 'careers forum' representatives may occasionally be asked to speak to parents and pupils about specialist fields of work. Under present conditions, the value of much of this is doubtful. For example in the study of working conditions, professional training in job analysis *is* essential, and teachers without this training are likely to make mistakes. Children are even more likely to make serious errors of judgment on the basis of a short visit or attachment to a workplace. They may well like the first impression of the attachment as a break in school routine; in a few careers programmes the author has seen such remarks as: 'After a few days' (attachment) 'she had liked the work' (in an office), 'and *decided to be a typist*' (my italics). Even if some preparation in ways of looking at jobs is given beforehand, children are unlikely to be able to make fair judgments on so little data, such small knowledge, and such limited experience of life.

*(b) Liaison with Parents*

Contact with parents is maintained by the visits of parents, usually to the school principal; by talks and 'parent evenings' held at the school, and, very occasionally, by visits by teachers to parents' homes. These may be fitted into a guidance scheme itself, for example in the term before specialist subjects are to be chosen by pupils, or in the main leaving year in the secondary modern school; or they may be combined with visits of business representatives to the school, so that pupils, parents and businessmen can meet. In the latter case a room may be prepared and set aside for a day or more, in which representatives from the working world can advertise. Or teachers and parents may meet on ceremonial occasions such as school speech days, or through parent-teacher association meetings. Finally, contact takes place indirectly through occasional correspondence, and. by regular formal reports on the progress of pupils. Outside school, informal meetings may take place between teachers and parents, but this is largely restricted to places where the school forms part of a closely knit community. With the exception of postal contact, none of the methods listed guarantees a meeting between the teacher and the problem parent—in particular with the parent from the lower working classes, who, as suggested earlier, may feel uncertain of himself outside his own social group. The author knows of no easy way to reach such people without the use of a more or less full time staff member trained in social work techniques, and has found no adequate answer in any school guidance programme. We shall be looking at the use of social workers in schools in the next chapter. Such specialist roles are hardly necessary for the cooperative parents, who attend parent-teacher association meetings and who answer letter No serious problems of communication arise with parents of this type.

Likewise the value of visitors and speakers to schools is suspect. Such people are often interested in selection rather than guidance, and may be seeking to recruit as big a body of applicants as possible, to draw off the best for their uses. In any case, it is probably very difficult for anyone to give an objective description of a career to which he is personally committed. The projection of a somewhat distorted image of work may harm, rather than help, the guidance effort.

Besides the above, some people might say that liaison with the working world is the proper business of the Youth Employment Officer, who is based outside the school and is continually in touch with job-placement. It was suggested earlier that these officers are often so overworked that they cannot be shouldered with the whole burden of such a task. Division of work in this area is best arranged locally by discussion with the officer concerned.

**Guidance Course Stages**

As schools and their pupils vary a good deal no rigid scheme of guidance can be laid down; but in the light of previous discussion a broad framework can be suggested, upon which many different programmes could be built. This basis would include:

(i) An initial period of assessment of the pupil, and of his environmental stresses and supports (home background, neighbourhood and friends).

(ii) A period of discussion between the individual pupil and the guidance teacher, during which the pupil gradually gets to know about himself, and matures in his outlook on his own future.

(iii) A period of individual and group exploration of the nature of post-school life, mediated by the teacher and the Youth Employment Officer, and possibly others.

These stages would not be separate. Assessment would go on throughout stages (2) and (3), partly to continue a study of his development', and partly to check the pupil's reaction to exposure to these later stages. Ideally, the length of each stage should be adjusted to meet the needs of the individual. In practice, the amount of work done must depend on the length of time given free to guidance staff, to the depth of their training, and to the staff-pupil ratio, Some guidance time could be worked into the academic timetable of other subjects, apart from the current testing of attainment level by normal school examination. Thus in stage (3) some aspects of post-school life could be studied by revising subject timetables, especially in the final year of an early leavers' group. Mathematics could include the study of handling income; the need for saving, and the difference between long-term and short-term expenditure; the calculation of income tax, and so on. English could include the analysis of job-advertisements, techniques of writing letters of application, and basic interview technique with mock interviews. In Geography, the influence of time-distance from work on the location of residence; the cost of emigration, and the differences between life in India Britain, Canada, the United States, and elsewhere. Some attention could also be given to basic sociological concepts, such as the effect of different living conditions on basic values of life. In History, the development and significance of the trade union movement could be dealt with.

No doubt the reader can think of many other examples directly relevant to the young worker's life, which might be included in a final school-year course. This sort of approach follows the recommendations of the Newsom Report that the last year of school should be made more meaningful for early leavers than at present.

Almost every aspect of guidance discussed above implies that a room or rooms should be available in the school as a centre for guidance work. The ideal structure of such a centre will vary from one school to another; but it should be a place reserved solely for guidance work, and not used as a common classroom, passageway, library or office. More ideally, two rooms are the ideal to aim at—a small guidance library used as a waiting room, and an adjoining office. This would house confidential documents, records, and master copies of careers literature. It should be equipped with a desk and comfortable chairs to fulfil its main use as an interviewing room, as well as with the usual storage faculties for confidential documents.

Realising the importance of guidance in the present day context, there should be proper arrangements for guidance in every institution. If to name it 'Guidance centre' it should be conveniently located at accessible place equipped with modern gadgets and communication facilities.

# 4

# Guidance in Primary and Higher Education

> "Virtue is not to be considered in the light of mere innocence, or abstaining from doing harm; but as the exertion of our faculties in doing good."
>
> —*Samuel Butler*

The need to provide adequate guidance for pupils in schools is certainly one of the critical unsolved problems. Three main reasons for this are the range of courses available to pupils, the wide spectrum of individual differences among applicants for them, and the size of the schools themselves. Exaggerations about the size of comprehensive have been common. In fact from 1955 to 1965 their average size remained pretty steady with around 970 pupils each. On the other hand the range of sizes is broad. Pedley (1964) found them to vary from 160 pupils to 2,150; and he noticed that many of the smaller schools were designed to grow to between 1,400 and 2,300. The problems of providing guidance increase sharply with the size of the school, and while we have worked out some hypothetical examples below for a school of 1,000 pupils, it is very likely that full time guidance specialists are needed in schools smaller than this. From recent work in the Keele area of Staffordshire, C.J. Gill estimates that 800 is the critical figure beyond which specialist guidance is advisable in any school; clearly the critical figure would vary with other factors, such as the amount of careers teaching which supporting staff could provide.

The range of courses available to any pupil at a comprehensive school normally increases with his age, frequently exceeding in diversity anything a normal grammar or secondary modern school can offer, extending from academic science through commerce and engineering to arts and business studies. Even the out of school activities of such places can be amazingly varied: for example Pedley gives a chart listing thirty different activities for a single school. The existence of so much to choose from, while offering to the pupil many opportunities absent elsewhere, adds enormously to his difficulties in making the right decision, and constitutes itself a decisive need for professional guidance.

As the comprehensive school accepts such a wide range of pupils, there is necessarily a wide range of differences in the level of work pupils can reach, as well as in intelligence, personal values, vocational aims, and home background. This probably accounts for the broad, scatter of leaving ages from these schools certainly comprehensive schools seem to meet the problems of the early, middle, and late leaver far more generally than do either secondary modern or grammar schools. Not only does this mean that vocational guidance programmes have to be complex and time consuming, but there are other problems too; we know from examples of comprehensive schools created by joining up local grammar and secondary modern schools that pupils are often drawn from many different social classes. This tendency is reflected in the scatter of leaving ages from comprehensive schools, which is extremely wide. There is a marked tendency for the greatest proportion of early leavers to come from the lower social classes, and of late leavers from middle classes, So in comprehensives we are likely to find many sociological problems due to the mingling of children at adolescence from very different home backgrounds, as well as a complex pattern of home background problems themselves. How many of our present teachers have received any training in dealing with parents from social classes other than their own? One wonders how many of them even understand the basic sociology of these problems. The fact that fairly extensive training is needed to equip social workers for dealing with these situations suggests the need for specialist guidance staff for this purpose alone.

Let us suppose that the distribution of measured intelligence is about the same in a comprehensive school of 1,000 pupils as in the population generally. Then some 160 could get scores low enough to rate them as subnormal, and of these about twenty-two could be classed as even more backward with I.Q.s below 70. Of course one should not define subnormality by the results of an I.Q. test alone. But a low I.Q. result like this always poses the question: Is this child subnormal? Why did he get a low score? It is simply not enough to shrug off the result of a carefully controlled objective test with sophisms about such things as social class and examination nerves. In fairness to the pupil, such a low result demands a careful further examination both of the test result and of the person. How stable is this low score? What parts of the test were clone particularly badly or well? Does such a low result agree with his academic record? How far does it agree with teachers' opinions about his ability? Are there abnormalities in his personality which might help to explain things? Is he for example unusually tense or dreamy? Is he bored with school? What is the state of his physical health? Has he home problems? Often these questions cannot adequately be answered by an amateur, or indeed by a professional with a heavy teaching load. In the example we have looked at, about 160 case studies of this sort would be needed following a routine I.Q. test of the school enrolment. This would mean getting to know the pupils individually through private talks and discussions; the administration, scoring and interpreting of a number of questionnaires; collating reports from the pupils' teachers; and in some cases visiting homes as well as obtaining detailed reports from the principals of former schools. Clearly there is enough work here to keep a full time guidance specialist busy. And of course this is only half the story: at the upper end of a normal distribution would lie a similar number of pupils apparently much brighter than the others. Probably fewer of these would need help because of personal difficulties, but what about the I.Q. 'genius' whose school work is much poorer than average? Or who is determined to leave school early and go and work in a factory on the production line?

What of those who are clearly maladjusted and in need of treatment? The incidence of such cases according to different studies in Britain has been found to vary from about 3% to nearly 12% among the child population. Taking this as a very rough guide, our school of 1,000 pupils could hold at any time between 30 and 120 children in need of professional psychological help, possibly over a long period of time; as we have seen earlier, the School Psychological Service is heavily overloaded and waiting lists of many weeks are common. No doubt some of these children would be included in the group of low I.Q.s we have just discussed, and perhaps among the high scorers as well, and it can be objected that the figures are estimates, and offer presumptive not direct evidence. But the estimates point at two uncomfortable conclusions; first, there is a great need for wide-scale research on the extent of serious maladjustment among the adolescent and pre-adolescent population generally, and in our new large comprehensive schools in particular; second, that very likely a ceiling of enrolment exists for every comprehensive school, beyond which a full time specialist is needed to deal with problem cases only. Although this ceiling is likely to vary markedly from place to place in a country of such intense regional differentiation.

Normal children manage to solve on their own the problems which in varying degrees incapacitate the abnormal;

this is because the problems are less intense, or the strength to overcome them is greater. These are the bulk of the school population for whom continuous guidance, systematic and varied assessment, and careful progress recording, are vital if they are to make the best use of their educational opportunities and to make wise vocational choices. In a comprehensive of 1,000 pupils the organisation and this work alone could occupy the whole time of one member of a guidance team. Suppose for example that, in keeping with the plan for continuous assessment, the children are all given an intelligence test and objective attainment tests in, say, English, Reading and Arithmetic in the first term. Using a group intelligence test such as Heim A.H., the total administrative time for each group would be 30-40 minutes, and possibly an average scoring time for each script would be five minutes; this would give sixteen hours of solid marking for a school intake of 200 pupils, for the I.Q. test alone, the simplest to score. Longer times would often be needed for attainment tests where judgment might be required on many scripts as well as mechanical scoring. Thus the total time might easily reach 100 hours. To balance these mainly objective tests with subjective impressions, to establish a personal relationship with the new pupils, and get some initial data about home background, an individual interview with each pupil might be a useful next step. Supposing that this could be kept to fifteen minutes each, with a further fifteen minutes for writing up each account immediately after the interview, another 100 hours of work would be required here. This does not take into account the time necessary to plan the interviews, get in touch with pupils and follow up the absentees. Interviewing of this sort could not be divided amongst other staff because this would defeat the aim of establishing a personal relationship with each pupil, and it would extend the error due to subjectivity. The adviser's further work, in interviewing older pupils, teaching and developing teaching courses for careers, building up a detailed record for each pupil, referring cases of maladjustment, and liaison with other specialists such as Youth Employment Officers, could easily provide sufficient work for a full time staff member in such a school.

Still many people, especially teachers, shrink from the idea of appointing full time guidance specialists. They feel that priority must be given to teaching; that full time guidance staff would have to be paid high salaries which could have provided more teachers to lessen the teaching load and reduce class sizes; and that the assessment, teaching and interviewing necessary would interfere with time-tabling and take up part of the school day. These points are valid, but the question seems to be whether we can do without such specialist help. After all, in some cases the 11 + is being abandoned not because it was a poor instrument of selection, but because from its results crude classifications into grammar, secondary modern, and other groups were made which ignored the individuality of the pupils. A major ideal of comprehensive education is to give individual development a better chance than before. The mistake in to assume that this will happen automatically by bringing general, grammar, and technical education together under one organisation. Pupils still have to select specialist subjects, or be selected for them; we do not get rid of the problems of selection itself with the abandonment of the 11 + ; we may however be in clanger of regressing to a system whereby selection is made according to the subjective opinions of teachers and others without the guidance of objective appraisal. The use of a more elaborate system of selection and guidance seems essential if these children are to be given the equal opportunities demanded by the comprehensive ideal. We may even have to consider the advisability, in very large schools, of appointing three or more full time experts—a teaching specialist to handle the organisation of careers work and assessment; a professional psychologist to handle abnormal problems of learning and adjustment; and a social worker to develop effective links between home and school. Such a team would not solve all guidance difficulties, as there might well be problems in its working organisation.

**Guidance in Primary Schools**

The extension of guidance into primary education can be justified, on the grounds that faults of learning and inadequacies of adjustment are better prevented than cured, and it is easier to do both in early life than later. But the concept of guidance in his area poses its own problems. In primary schools on the other hand, the children are much younger, more dependent, and spend most of the working day under the influence of one teacher. We have to consider if this setting is the right one for guidance work, if the class teacher is already adequately trained for such work, and if not, what changes might be possible. The role of the class teacher under the present system gives him undoubted advantages as a potential guidance specialist. He is much better placed than his successor in the secondary school to get to know the child at first hand, "and he is the teacher normally consulted by the school principal about the promotion, streaming, or transfer of pupils in his class.

Teachers who handle the same class for long periods may tend to develop prejudices about pupils. McIntyre, Morrison and Sutherland (1966) selected' thirty-four teachers of 11-12 year olds in primary schools in a Scottish city and studied their ratings of pupils' personality traits and attainments. Some main findings were that teachers in middle class and mixed social class schools specially valued the pleasant and trustworthy pupil, whilst those in urban and suburban working class schools valued the hard-working or clever pupil more. Older and more experienced teachers valued persistence, enthusiasm and high attainment in their pupils, whilst the younger teachers were better pleased by children who behaved themselves in class. There were also sex distinctions, girls being generally seen in a more stereotyped way than boys. Thus the meaning of the 'ideal' pupil, or the pupil 'worth taking trouble over' varied" with the age and experience of the teachers, the social class background of schools, and the sex of the pupils. If the close relationship established with pupils through primary classroom teaching is not enough to counter errors of subjective judgment, such teachers may not be able to fulfil an adequate guidance role unless they are capable of using objective tests to balance their own opinions. Here, unfortunately, is where we find a serious inadequacy in the teacher training system.

Very few primary teachers are qualified to use aptitude tests, intelligence tests, or attitude surveys of a standardised nature. This is not the fault of the colleges of education which train the teachers, for, as explained in this study, there are insuperable difficulties to attaching all students to schools for the experience necessary for such qualifications. But the problem becomes more serious as time goes on, for with the increasing recognition of the importance of guidance in primary schools, sophisticated programmes for such purposes are now appearing. An example is that recently constructed by Norman France and Stephen Wiseman (1966), designed to measure in primary schools different aspects of intellect and personality, and to provide a comprehensive picture of the child as a whole. Prepared for successive use over first, second and third years in such schools, its sub-tests range from conventional ones such as addition/ subtraction, spelling, and composition, to spatial reasoning, picture completion, likes and dislikes, and attitudes to the family. A great deal of work has gone into the statistical basis of the test, including for example a consideration of regional differences in scoring patterns. But the value of this would be wasted were the test, to be used by someone who could not interpret its standardisation data, lacked training in the administration of such tests, or, worst of all, misjudged the results through ignorance of the nature and limitations of such instruments. It will indeed be a pity if our research workers continue to turn out a succession of refined guidance aids such as this, which cannot be used because of a shortage of trained staff in the schools.

Further, primary school teachers have little opportunity during the working day to make adequate contact with guidance agencies outside the school. They have fewer free periods than their colleagues in secondary schools, and this also limits their usefulness for such specialist work. One partial solution to this would be to select from the ranks of existing teachers those who because of outstanding personal qualities are suited for guidance work, and delegate this to them with a lightened teaching load. It is true that here and there among teachers one meets individuals who have that gift of warmth and understanding which makes it easy for adults and children, alike to put caution aside for once and speak straight from the heart; but their numbers art too few. Perhaps this is an argument for training selected students at colleges of education in the principles and techniques of guidance with the idea that after some full time teaching experience they combine an advisory service to teachers in individual primary schools with a limited teaching role. But in contrast to the position in secondary schools, the status of the classroom teacher in primary education seems to make it inevitable that the main work of guidance should be done by him. It account in any future planning for the extension.

**Guidance in Higher Education**

The work of universities and colleges of education is fairly clearly defined, but a third group, Institutions of Further Education, includes many different establishments from polytechnics offering degree courses, to local colleges providing general education beyond school leaving age and largely concerned with training junior technicians, craftsmen, and other workers. The term also covers art schools, colleges of commerce, agricultural colleges, and such specialised institutions as the College of Aeronautics at Cranfield and the Royal College of Art.

There is a very wide range of problems in this field, some of which arise at least in part through the educational system itself. For example many of our most able students spend their last years in secondary education preparing for entry to universities, and then, after obtaining the necessary minimum qualifications for entry, find that they cannot obtain a place.

The Robbins Report found that between 1954 and 1961 the percentage of the age group obtaining minimum university-entrance requirements rose from 4.3% to 6.9%, whereas the percentage managing to achieve university entrance rose from 3.2% to only 4.1%. In a report for the Advisory Centre for Education, Newton and Abrams (1965) noted that in 1962, 27% of the applicants with minimum university entrance requirements were unable to obtain a place: in absolute numbers, 8,650. In fact the universities, faced with many more applicants than they can take, appear to have been skimming the cream of the examination successes. Labovitch (1965) has pointed out that in that year about 80% of English and Welsh university students had at least three passes in A level examinations, and about half of them had passed with marks of 60% or more in at least two subjects. The frustration which many otherwise successful students feel at failing to get into a university is aggravated by the element of gambling involved in the selection system, which makes applying for entry to a university rather like playing the pools. This begins with the initial steps necessary in making application. With a few exceptions, the normal method is to apply through the Universities Central Council for Admissions (UCCA). This system allows the applicant to name six universities of his choice, and to adopt a number of different strategies for declaring preference. Various unknown factors are thus allowed a chance to work. Universities rated as first preference by a student may be inclined to view the applicant more favourably than those with lower ratings, but those lower an the list may be the easier to enter. Newton and Abram:; (1965) in advising students about university application, point out that students likely to be in the borderline group might find it advisable to choose a university as first preference where the demand for places is less intense. The element of gambling has been noted specifically by Bochm who writes: 'This the UCCA form completion") is not simple, especially from the point of view of the gamesmanship of University entrance.' Some of the blame for the injustices of the entrance system can be attributed to the reactions of universities themselves. This point has been made forcefully by Labovitch (1965) who writes: '[The Universities] choose whom they please; moreover, to make the problem more inscrutable still, each university shrouds its selection techniques in mystery. Thus a candidate who has been turned down by two or three universities may suddenly be accepted by a university which was supposedly the most competitive of all. In part this inconsistency arises from differences attached to the candidate's non-academic record. It also springs from the non-scientific nature of the interview.' Not much is known yet about the overall pattern of stress affecting students in higher education. The percentage of students who need help in difficulties can only be guessed.

Malleson (1963) estimated that at London University between 1% and 2% of the students would develop serious psychiatric trouble during their undergraduate courses; about 15% would need help with personal problems, and of these about a quarter would need lengthy help. Furneaux (1962) suggested that an average of 25% of students would need help, and in a later study of London University students,

Kelvin, Lucas and Ojha (1965) found that no fewer than 40% of a random sample of 147 students came to doctors of the Student Health Association with complaints of distress during their courses. In a college of further education, Claude Palmer (1965) found a level of disturbance roughly the same as that described by Malleson for university students. Little seems to be known as yet about the incidence of distress in other places, for example in colleges of education. G. W. Miller (1968) has suggested a possible overall picture. Accepting that about 15% of the student population in universities will develop neuroses and/or psychotic episodes, he estimates a total of 30,000 students at risk for the whole of Britain, and 50,000 including students in other forms of higher education. He emphasizes that this takes no account of the much larger proportion who may need timely assistance with less severe though potentially serious difficulties which might affect academic performances and mental health if disregarded.

Palmer (1965) has dealt in some detail with descriptions of the sort of problems he encountered among students at a college of further' education. He found it impossible to define any single cause for maladjustment; among those which he mentions as occurring frequently are anxieties arising from the lack of value systems among students; lack of money and of an environment conducive to study; from sexual relationships; from relationships with tutors; and from parent-student relationships. Along with Malleson (who reported on university students) he found that stress could arise from a 'decompression syndrome'—the group of symptoms which develop when a bright pupil, who has been helped and encouraged by his teachers, is placed in higher education where he misses the frequent injections of confidence from teachers, and the support of home life. Among problems brought to me by students in a college of education in Lancashire, difficulties in relationships with parents were very common. It would be interesting to know how such patterns of problems vary from one institution to another.

A major current source of stress among students, especially in colleges of education, seems to centre upon the failure of the college authorities to accord them the rights and privileges of adults. The nature of restrictions which students find most irksome have been suggested in a survey of nearly all Local Education Authority colleges of education in England and Wales (Phillips, 1966). Many of these colleges are residential, and students often found residence in hall unsuitable. In a number of colleges students were not however allowed to take a fiat rather than a room in a hall of residence. In over 95% of the colleges restrictions were placed on the time of entry into halls at right, the average time being from 10.30 to 11 p.m. About 28% of colleges restricted weekend leave, and this was a major source of frustration. Free visiting of men and women in each others' rooms was generally forbidden; although only 17% forbade such visiting completely, in the remaining colleges the time allowed was often very limited. Students also objected generally to the number of hours of compulsory lectures attendance, and the report recommended that students should be given the right to attend lectures at their own discretion. Restrictions of an obviously unreasonable nature were rare, and in the colleges staff/student relations were generally good; but there were occasional exceptions to this; for example in a few colleges students generally described the regulations as 'silly and childish'; in five of the seventy-three colleges surveyed there was a bar on political societies. In justice to the colleges as a whole, it should be said that this rather authoritarian picture is relieved by a few of the most outstanding colleges, where the opportunities for staff-student consultation and the atmosphere of liberality compare favourably with many universities.

Restrictions of the sort outlined above act as a kind of forced guidance, or rather of direction, as they arbitrarily define right from wrong behaviour and in effect try to shape the individual into the mould of a pre-conceived ideal person.

They are not peculiar to colleges of education; as Professor Taylor (1967) notes, similar restrictions occur in theological colleges and in the Oxbridge foundations. On the other hand, under the pressure of contemporary events many colleges and universities have been moving towards a more liberal outlook on student freedom.

Now taking the case of Essex University, which admitted its first students in 1964, deliberately intended to break the tradition which places universities *in loco parents*. To achieve its purpose as a community of learning it was felt that students should be treated as partners and adults; and that to give responsibility to students was the best way to encourage development. Basic to the treatment of students as adults is the freedom granted to them, regardless of age or year, to live in accommodation of their own choice, either inside the university or in lodgings, bedsitters, flats or houses in the surrounding area. This freedom is reflected in the nature of the university accommodation itself. This is in towers of fourteen stories each. Except for the top two floors which contain separate flats for graduates, married students and staff, each floor of the tower is a flat with its own front door. Each comprises cooking, toilet, and washing facilities, with furnished bed-sitting' rooms and study rooms. Residents and non-residents have equal rights of access, and men and women are accommodated in the same tower, the flats for men alternating with those for women. Apart from the tower's maintenance and rent-collection, each one is run by a committee of management made up from people in each flat. A research study of one of these towers was made by Clossick (1967) during the year 1965-1966, to find how the tower system was functioning not as an isolated building, but as part of the university. She found that the freedom and independence were widely appreciated; the atmosphere seemed more adult than that of many ether student residences, and there was no clear evidence that students living there studied more or less, or did worse or better in examinations than non-residents. The research in particular showed that the tower was operating as an open rather than a closed community; there was little pressure to have a friend of the opposite sex, to do a certain amount of work and no more; students frequently were found to have boy or girl friends outside the university.

Professor Taylor (1967) believes that in his country we are seeing signs of a desire on the part of student to return to the original German conception of academic freedom, with an absence of administrative coercions in the learning situation, freedom for students to determine the choice and sequence of courses, and of attendance at them; exemption from all tests except the final examination; and freedom to live in private quarters and control their own lives. But he also suggests that while this movement has enhanced the freedom of the student to live and study in the way he chooses, it may be doing so at the cost of removing much of the personal concern and interest in the development of the student that used to be shown by more authoritarian educational institutions. It may be that as pressures of conformity upon students diminish, a greater need for guidance on a voluntary basis will appear. Some attempt at this is already provided in many universities and other colleges.

Sir Edward Hale (1967) has provided some data from the results of a Universities Grants Committee of which he was chairman, which questioned a wide sample of undergraduates about the frequency with which they had discussions with a person assigned to organise their studies or to give advice on them. Seventy-eight% of the, students had such supervision; 36% saw their studies adviser at least once a week; 9% once a fortnight, and 17% once or twice a term. The remaining 38% were either unassigned, or met their supervisors for discussion less often than once a term. There were wide differences between universities. At Oxford and Cambridge 93% of students had a supervisor whom they saw at least once a week. In the Scottish universities the corresponding percentage was only 8, and 74% were unassigned or met their tutors rarely. Elsewhere differences between these extremes occurred. Colleges of education generally also appoint studies advisers, and there seem to be wide differences here also in the frequency of consultations.

It seems probable that in many cases the advisers appointed do not have specialist qualifications in guidance, and the practice of allocating small numbers of students to individual members of staff on this basis, who are expected to provide this service when required, is an inadequate solution to present day needs. Many universities and colleges now provide at least one full time guidance specialist, as well as specialist such as psychiatrists. The development of guidance personnel teams along these lines seems to offer a more hopeful prospect for the individual happiness of students in large and complex organisations in near future.

**Summing Up**

In most fields of education there is room for full time guidance specialists attached to schools and other educational institutions. In many cases the need is urgent, and is reflected by the heavy pressure on Youth Employment Officers and School Psychologists. Much research has yet to be done on the nature of pupil and student difficulties, and on the patterns of their development. There are also, however, many problems concerned with the working of guidance teams themselves, and with the selection and training of people for them.

Coming to Indian case, we lack in this field miserably. Despite urgent need of guidance services, at schools, we have to made a long and arduous journey.

## *REFERENCES*

A.F. Hinrichs (Chief Economist, U.S. Bureau of Labor Statistics), *Trends of Employment Opportunity*, pp. 14-18.

Charles F. Roos, *The Dynamics of Automobile Demand*, p. 95.

Francis Spaulding, *High School and Life*, McGraw-Hill Book Co., Inc., New York, 1938.

Harold G. Campbell, *Report of Superintendent of Schools*, Board of Education, City of New York, 1934, pp. 31-33.

Symposium, "New Frontiers in American Life," *New York Herald-Tribune*, May 7, 1940.

Symposium, "The Opportunity for Youth in Building the World of Tomorrow," *The New York Times*, May 7, 1940.

# 5

# Training for Guidance

"Better to do right from wrong motives, than wrong from right motives. Whether you lose your own soul is not significant, but how your acts affect others is of vital importance."

—*E.W. Helms*

If guidance involved no more than giving vocational information when it was asked for, and to the extent that it was asked for, it might be possible to programme a computer to do this, and to use it as a kind of central clearing house for all enquiries from a given area. If it involved only the gradual exposure of groups of children to concepts of the world of work and to a selected range of occupations, we might train some of our better teachers as guidance specialists in such a setting. But as we have seen in this study, the work also means helping individuals, some of them children, some parents, in the resolution of personal problems of many different kinds which are intimately interwoven with their personal decisions. This is a process of counselling, and it is important that we do not select and train people who have little aptitude or interest in handling such interpersonal situations.

To our utter dismay, the question of what sort of person is best fitted for a counselor role has not yet been solved. One reason for this is that we do not yet know what factors in the counselling situation are most decisive in helping the client. Is it the warmth and understanding of the therapeutic relationship? Is it a matter of giving the client the right information at the right time? Is it the ability on the part of the counselor to develop and maintain a client-centred relationship? Probably the right approach varies with the kind of problems, and different clients probably also require changing approaches. Again, if we accept that guidance involves more than crisis counselling, that it means helping the client to define his personal values, then unless the counselor can remain completely impersonal, his own values are likely to play some part in shaping those of his client. This raises the question of what values are most appropriate for counselling, and underlines the complexity of the concept of guidance, and of the choice of personnel for it.

**Ideal Counsellor**

Cottle (1953), quoting findings about counselors in American secondary education, gives the following list of identified characteristics: fairness, sincerity, 'personality', good character and wholesome philosophy, common sense, health, emotional stability, approachability, ability to get along with people, sympathetic .understanding of youth, interest in people, understanding people different: from one's own self, flexibility and adaptability, intelligence and mental alertness, social culture, broad knowledge and interests, leadership, awareness of one's own limitations, professional attitude, sense of mission, interest in guidance and personnel work, understanding of classroom conditions, understanding of working conditions, and understanding of social and economic conditions. Cottle goes on to point out that some of these are more matters of knowledge than personal qualities, and that several of them are ambiguous and open to misinterpretation. It is apparent also that such lists largely represent the subjective opinions of the people who make them, and that it would be very difficult to distinguish on such a basis between counselors and other school personnel. Cottle also notes that when lists compiled in this way by different researchers are compared, the qualities vary so much hat it is difficult to select any list that represents a common measure of agreement.

Some rather more objective evidence has been obtained through the use of psychometric tests. Arbuckle (1958), in a study of trainees who had been chosen or rejected by their fellows as potential counselors, found that on the Kuder Vocational Interest Inventory, the 'chosen' group scored higher than the 'rejected' group on Social Service, Persuasive; Literary and Scientific interests. He also mentions a study by W.V. Snyder, who found that 'good' students were more aggressive, independent, unconventional, intellectual and social, and were less religious. On the other hand 'poor students tended to have feelings of inadequacy and neurotic concerns. fligh Kuder scores on Literary and Social Service scales, as well as on the Persuasive Interest scale, were also found by DiMichael (1949) in a study on vocational rehabilitation counselors. DiMichael also found that such counselors obtained low scores on Mechanical, Computational, Scientific, Artistic and Clerical Interest scales. Although such attempts at objective measurement may eventually prove a useful help for selection, they have not yet been thoroughly explored. One notes, for example, that while both DiMichael and Arbuckle obtained high interest scores for counselors on Literary, Social; Service and Persuasive Interests, the studies provided conflicting evidence about scientific interests.

Wrenn (1952) obtained high scores on the Theoretical and Religious scale of the Allport-Vernon-Linrizey Study of Values in a survey of graduate counselor trainees, which is apparently at variance with some of the results found by Snyder. These contradictions may be more apparent than real, due perhaps to the use of different tests with different samples, but they point to the need for further research.

Attempts have been made to summarize the difficulties of selecting counselors. A synopsis of these has been made in America by Hill (1961). While directed towards a limited group, the reader will see that many of his conclusions might well apply to the role of the guidance specialist in British schools. He lists these difficulties:

1. The variety of roles and relationships involved in the work of any one counselor.
2. The diversity of skills, understandings, interests, and attitudes expected in a counselor from one school to another, together with evidence that even in North America counselors are often asked to carry out duties which have little or no relationship to the specialist role for which they have been trained.
3. The wide range of individual differences among counselors, reflected in research studies which have so far failed to show a standard personality pattern for them.
4. The existence of a hierarchy of guidance positions. Thus the necessary personal characteristics of the successful careers teacher in Britain nay be different from those required, say, by the school psychologist or teacher/social worker. Cottle (1953) had touched on this point earlier, saying that it was not clear whether the same characteristics were required for the successful counselor in the elementary (primary) school as for the secondary school or college.

Hobbs believes that the 'compleat counselor' should be a competent technician, in diagnosis, therapy and research, including such aspects as the use of psychological tests. Few would deny the need for these basic skills. Second, he should be a goad psychologist. The need for a thorough grounding in psychology is obviously necessary, even as part of the process of becoming technically competent. Third, he should be a good teacher, partly because his work will mainly be in schools, and other 'educational institutions, and partly to avoid ultra-professionalism. Some of these three basic requirements match very closely, as we shall see below, with the qualifications required for entry to the university counselling courses now being offered in some British institutes of education, and others with the content of these training courses. Hobbs' most interesting idea, however, stems from his conviction that modern society is changing so swiftly, both economically and socially, that counselors cannot discharge their responsibilities effectively with-out being aware of these trends, and having personal value systems which enable them to meet such rapidly changing conditions. He holds that the essence of success here is creativity of thought, which while allowing the counselor to master convenient scientific aids to guidance, such as the use of psychometrics, learning theory, and client centred counselling, prevents him from becoming their slave.

He says:

> The counselor whose entire personal security system, in and out of counseling, is bound up in some particular construct system, is a very limited person indeed and a deterrent to progress in the field... we should attempt to attract to the field of counseling bright young people from a variety of backgrounds. Our least promising candidate for training might be a person who has dutifully plodded through undergraduate majors in psychology and education. And our most exciting candidates might be people with very odd backgrounds, or people whose non-conforming tendencies, particularly in the realm of ideas, have gotten them into trouble elsewhere.

In many ways Hobbs' views echo those of Wrenn in his book *The Counselor in a Changing World.* Similarly, Tyler (1961) has stressed that rather than defining too closely what to look for in a good counselor, one should look for what to avoid, and especially to note rigidity of thought in a candidate. Among other pointers, 'this shows itself in an inability to tolerate ambiguity and uncertainty, the need to be sure of using the right technique, and in expecting a client to respond in specified ways. Although the conclusion is not certain, it is probable that conformists display this defect more often than non-conformists.

**Selection and Training of Guidance Personnel**

*(1) Selection*

Advanced courses in counselling and guidance, lasting throughout one academic year, are offered at "present within the Institutes of Education of Reading, Exeter, and Keele Universities, and a similar course at Swansea is in preparation. Candidates must be qualified teachers and have completed a minimum of between three and five years' teaching. In addition, all three universities carry out further selection procedures. Without exception a quality looked for among candidates is flexibility, shown in different ways, as in the ability to talk to people who are specialists in various subjects and to ask the right kind of questions. It is also shown in a sympathetic and kind approach to pupils. All courses also look for candidates who can mix readily with children and adults, are fairly popular with staff and pupils, and integrate their own approach with those of other people. Creativity is also sought after. Individual universities also stress such factors as abstract and verbal ability, good physical health, extra-curricular activity, reliability, organizing ability, and low emotionality.

Clearly no well defined criteria of selection have as yet been found, and a wide not is cast in the qualities looked for. But there seems to be a fair agreement on the need to avoid the prosaic, rigid-minded sort of person condemned by writers such as Hobbs and Tyler. There seems to be common agreement also that even if the counselor does not teach, he should be acceptable as a teacher to school stall through prior training and experience; if this becomes the future pattern it may help to avoid come of the dangers of ultra-professionalism mentioned by Hobbs.

*(2) Content of Course*

The three universities have many features in common. Guidance is studied in relation to contemporary issues, social and philosophical, in British education; an important part of each course is given to studying educational psychology, and the development of normal and abnormal characteristics in children; each has further major sections on statistical measurement, the principles and practice of psychometric testing, their use in guidance, and the use of systems for recording the individual development of children. Finally each course requires its candidates to do a certain amount of practical work. This varies from straight-forward guidance work in schools to studies of role playing, supervised counselling interviews using tape-recorders and one-way mirrors, and attachments to hospitals, welfare organisations and child guidance clinics.

The courses have certain common principles, such as the view that crisis-counselling is undesirable, and that guidance techniques, and use modern psychometric tests and recording systems. They all have a broad base of studies extending from theories of education through practical training to the speculative issues of counselling. There can be little doubt that with so much in common they will influence the evolution of future counselling courses in other universities and institutions of higher education in the United Kingdom. They suggest also that the trend in Britain may be to require school counselors to be qualified teachers. The National Association of School Counselors has recently been formed, its membership restricted to successful students of these university courses. A survey carried out by the Schools Council in 1966 showed that the majority of those who passed the courses had in fact gained posts as full or part time school counselors notably with the Local Education Authority of Stoke-on-Trent. Also, G.D. Moore and J. B. Fuller (1967) carried out a survey of the roles of eighteen counselors who qualified at Reading in 1966. Nearly all of these had returned to school work after their courses. Half of them took up posts where about 50 per cent of their time was for counselling work. In general they had been well received in their new roles, no serious problems of communication had arisen with educational psychologists or other agencies, and in several schools the counselors had been asked to co-ordinate the work of guidance agencies outside the school.

The main centre for research in guidance and counselling is the Vocational Guidance Research Unit at Leeds. At Manchester University the Department of Social Administration is concerned with the Central Lancashire Family and Community Project whose object is to carry out experimental preventative and remedial services and to do research on the interaction between school and society. These are mentioned here because their work brings them into close contact with the universities already referred to, although they do not run specific training courses of their own. Undergraduate and post-graduate training for educational and clinical psychologists is of course provided by many universities; at Edinburgh however the Applied Psychology Unit has functions which bring it closer to the field of vocational guidance. In addition to giving honours psychology students and some others practical training in basic psychological skills, a small scale service in vocational and educational guidance is provided for the general public. Students are thus given an opportunity of observing at close quarters vocational guidance in practice, and of trying to relate their theoretical knowledge to the problem in hand. The Unit also carries out research in vocational guidance, selection and related topics.

## Guidance Courses at Colleges of Education

Training in some aspects of guidance, and in the principles of psychological testing, forms an integral part of many of the education courses which are compulsory for student teachers at colleges of education. It is however very difficult for these colleges to offer full training in guidance work to all students. We have seen that, schools with effective guidance programmes are rare, and there would be insuperable problems in attaching hundreds of students from a single college to observe those available at work. And while school principals are normally willing to allow students to practise using standardised tests with pupils, some principals are very reluctant to allow the student and pupils to discuss results. In the words of one school head, such discussion might lead to criticism of the school or of individual staff.

One finds colleges which offer courses in guidance techniques to a few interested and suitable students. The first to start training specifically in vocational guidance was Edge Hill College in Lancashire, where an optional course, taken in the second and third years of training, has been offered since 1965. This course is not designed to produce specialists in guidance, but to make a few teachers in training more aware of the current need for such specialists, and of their approach and methods. But it is anticipated that some of those completing the course may later become careers teachers, or go on to one of the university counselling courses. Criteria for selection have been kept very general, because of the uncertainties already outlined. Students must, of course, have already been accepted for training as teachers, and have completed satisfactorily the first year of their college course; preference *is* given to those who have some experience of the world of work between leaving school and starting college; and to those whose first year has been satisfactory from the viewpoint of academic and teaching progress; underlying this is an assumption that a weak teacher is unlikely to be acceptable to staff as a good careers teacher. The programme of studies is similar to that of the universities, but the students' commitments to other courses at college limit the time available for practical work. Visits to schools, short attachments to factories and offices, including Youth Employment Offices, form part of the course, and are partly completed in the vacations. A programme of evening visits to youth clubs, dance halls, coffee bars, discotheques and elsewhere is compulsory, and the students are asked to mix as freely as possible with the young people there, and to find out as much as they can about their vocational aims, attitudes, and the amount of careers work which they did at school, as well as the kind of guidance which they received there. In 1965 the college began in-service training in careers guidance for qualified teachers, and at present runs two successive courses of one term each, annually, on a modified form of the two-year curriculum. In 1967 a course in Educational Development was introduced. for selected students, who study it in the first and second years of their training. This was designed to make students more aware of the problems of guidance in primary schools, and to extend their experience of interviewing younger children, and using a small array of psychological tests. Rather more time has been devised for practical work in this course than in the two-year course already outlined. The course lays emphasis upon the need for guidance in primary education, a field which even in North America has not been as fully developed as in their high school system.

Although such courses are very rare in other colleges of education, a larger number offer training in youth work or in social work, so that interested students will be qualified, in addition to their careers as teachers, to take posts as Youth Club leaders, or to carry out diagnostic work with problem families for later referral to social workers. A list of the colleges which offer such courses is contained in the Schools

Council Report mentioned earlier, and in the A.T.C.D.E. Annual Handbook of Colleges and Departments of Education.

**Training for Guidance**

The main centres for guidance training have been described above. However growing interest in training has been reflected by a number of short courses organised in recent years through the Department of Education and Science. These have lasted for about a week each, and have been designed to show practising teachers and others some of the recent trends and problems in the field. Many institutes and departments up and down the country also organize local lectures and short courses in guidance. This is a pattern which is rapidly changing with the increasing demand for knowledge about guidance. To help meet this, the Department has now ceased to run its own courses, and instead is encouraging Local Education Authorities them-selves to organize similar courses on a regional basis, with help provided through H.M. Inspectors.

**Summing Up**

The trend in guidance today is towards replacement of the amateur by the professional. No doubt this is partly in recognition of the importance of the subject, but it also stems from an awareness of the damage which can be caused by indifference or by the wrong sort of approach. The emphasis in the new courses seems to be on centering guidance in schools, and on giving additional training to teachers. There are very good reasons for this, and these have been discussed at length in the present book. Two fields however remain comparatively undeveloped. These are, training for guidance specifically in primary schools, and the education of parents in the new approaches. A start might be possible in the first area through extension of courses along the lines of those now emerging. The second need might be partly met by the wider use of radio and television programmes. It should be possible to illustrate examples of many aspects of guidance, such as counselling techniques, the way in which psychological tests can be used, and the idea of guidance as a continuous process, in a far more vivid way than by any system of lectures. The problem of the really uncooperative parent will still remain, but at present one suspects that even interested and highly intelligent people are often almost totally in the dark about the use of many new ideas in guidance.

# 6

# Education and Vocational Guidance

> "Bodily exercises, when compulsory, do harm to the body; but knowledge which is acquired under compulsion obtains no hold on the mind."
>
> —*Plato*

Vocational guidance can be expressed as helping people to choose work in which they will be reasonably contented, and successful within the limits of their abilities. It involves the idea of guidance towards a career which will be completely absorbing, to a life that will be fulfilled by work—i.e., a vocation. In both cases, vocational happiness requires that a person's interests, aptitudes and personality be suitable for his job (occupation).

Significantly, the need for vocational guidance for young people today is probably greater than it has ever been in the past anywhere. From the academic viewpoint this has been made clear through the writings of sociologists and social psychologists such as Thelma Veness, Peter Daws, Michael Carter, R.V. Clements and many more; and from the professional viewpoint by the appearance at a number of universities of diploma courses in counselling and guidance for qualified teachers.

Vocational guidance has even appeared as a profitable financial business, suggested by the emergence of a number of firms offering specialist advice for a fee. The reasons for this need cannot be explained in a few pages, but they clearly lie in the increasing educational opportunities of the century, the wide range of possible occupations offered by our complex society, in the rapidity of industrial change, and in the disintegration of old principles and certainties which formerly guided important decision making before the great economic, social and political upheavals of the last two centuries. We shall survey briefly the main agencies providing guidance and look at the pattern of their development, and we shall discuss some of the most important issues now facing us. These will include the problem of how far schools should be involved in guidance, and in what ways; how the various guidance services might be brought together for more effective work; how closer links might be forged between the home and the school; and how guidance specialists are to be selected and trained.

This would be impractical, since new ideas and policies are appearing almost every month. The field of guidance field is expanding—almost exploding—into recognition after many decades of stagnation. But the answers to its deeper problems come more slowly. Such questions as how far we have the right to suggest vocational goals to our adolescents; what moral principles should influence our suggestions; how far we should encourage an individual to develop his own goals in life if these do not match the economic needs of the State; how far we have the right to invade the privacy of the individual in our search for his pattern of aptitudes, interests, and the forces shaping his vocational decisions; how such information should be stored to protect the privacy of the individual; the nature of the interpersonal relationship which makes it possible for a guidance specialist to help a person; what personal qualities we should look for in selecting candidates for training as guidance specialists; and how inter - professional jealousies and suspicions might be eased in building up guidance teams—these important questions are likely to remain unresolved for many years. They emerge in the present book sometimes directly, and sometimes by implication as factors underlying the guidance systems which we discuss. Occasional answers suggest themselves, but the overall picture is still one of open enquiry. As the current disturbances among young people suggest, they are of the first importance to the parents, teachers, social workers and students of guidance.

When a person opts for a career, he is making a decision as important as his choice of close friends, of a wife, or of a way of living. This is something that cannot be done lightly or in a short space of time—say during the last year at school. One reason why early guidance is important is that many children do not look upon their first job as the start of a career, but as something much less important. Michael Carter (1966) has suggested that possibly one half of the children in our secondary modern schools come from families where both education and work are thought of with apathy, and where parents' knowledge of both is very limited, and his conclusion is supported by the later evidence of the Schools Council Enquiry on Young School Leavers (1968). Another reason is that by the time an adolescent has reached school leaving age he is already limited in his choice of jobs by what he has already learned, especially when his secondary education has involved specialisation in certain subjects for any length of time. For example a boy reaching O level in English, History, Geography, French and Art, who then decided that he wished to become a doctor, would be at an immediate disadvantage through his ignorance of scientific subjects. At this stage—i.e., O level—there is a wide range of careers which, if not closed, are difficult for all but a small percentage of people to enter. These are grounds for thinking that vocational guidance should be concerned with individual choice of specialist subjects at an early stage of the secondary school course, as well as with the later transition stage from school to work.

One of the chief aims of secondary education should be to continue a liberal education started in the primary school, and that whatever subjects are chosen for specialisation, they should promote the 'liberal' idea. The difficulty is that no general agreement exists as to what subject make up the basis of a liberal education. Few people would agree today with the sentiments of Jean - Pierre Hebart: 'Nothing is better fitted to impart a taste for free thought, sound judgment and criticism than the exercise of translating the ancient languages. Yet one still finds people who maintain that a sound knowledge of the mechanics of English grammar helps fluent expression and thought, in spite of the absence of any scientific evidence to support this argument. Likewise there are many who believe that team games are good for the development of character and a spirit of selflessness and cooperation: indeed games form an important part of the tradition of the English Public School system, although here too there is little evidence to support the view.

There are certain subjects of outstanding importance at primary school level which children must master if they are to maintain the means of communication within the society. But in secondary education is there not something wrong in the assumption that any single subject has more value than another? Definitely it is less the subject itself than the way in which it is presented, and the breadth and depth of its teaching, that give it significance? Moreover the value of any subject will vary from individual to individual at different periods of life, a view presented eloquently during this century by A.N. Whitehead and Sir Percy Nunn. Perhaps adolescents should be given more freedom to choose the subjects they wish to study in accordance with their own aptitudes and interests, and not to meet the dictates of any pre - arranged curriculum. No doubt they should be encouraged to think also of the significance of such subjects to the future pattern of their lives. Fortunately he trend in education seems to be in this direction; the spread of comprehensive secondary schools greatly widens the range of subjects which can be offered to pupils once they have reached the stage of specialisation. In some of these schools the idea that educational and vocational guidance are part of the same process has already been accepted, and elaborate carefully planned guidance systems are appearing.

Once it has been recognised that vocational guidance involves educational guidance as well, the system of giving vocational advice towards the end of school life may be extended by adding an earlier stage of advice. This might be done at the time when decisions have to be made regarding the choice of specialist subjects, usually at the end of the second or third year in grammar schools, and the writer has seen a number of school programmes in which this is the pattern. But even a simple two - stage process is difficult to work successfully without going further into the concept of what guidance involves. First there is the problem of helping the adolescent to discover what subjects are best suited to his particular aptitudes and interests. The advice of teachers and parents here may be valuable, but as we shall see in the next chapter, it may be based on limited experience and coloured by prejudices of which neither is aware. Psychological tests and questionnaires may throw more light on the matter, but they too can lead to difficulties when used in schools. First, they can be dangerously misleading if used by unqualified staff, and for this reason their issue is generally restricted to those with suitable training. Second, they give an essentially static picture of the individual and during the rapid changes that take place in adolescence such tests given at the age of, say, fourteen, do not always show the way in which development will take place during the next few years.

To do this, they have to be repeated at intervals throughout the secondary school period, and the results compared.

Third, there is the difficulty of explaining their use to the pupil, and of obtaining his support and the co - operation of his parents. The work of getting apathetic or resistant parents to modify their attitudes towards education and the future of their children may itself take a long time, and perhaps require the use of a teacher specially trained in social work to bridge the gap between home and school. The two - stage guidance system also has the disadvantage that it does not educate the individual towards making successful decisions in a rapidly changing environment. Economic and social forces are altering the nature of our society so swiftly that no one can foresee what the pattern of employment will be in two decades from now. This theme has been graphically treated from the American viewpoint by Gilbert Wrenn in "The Counselor in a Changing World", and he suggests that the safe solutions to the problems of today may spell disaster later on, unless individuals have been taught how to cope with far - reaching changes in their surroundings. The same point was made in Britain in the N.F.E.R. Statement of Policy in 1953. Later M.W. Thring (1965) has suggested that a working week of twenty hours might be envisaged in the future, and that consequently more education for leisure is needed. In practice this means that adolescents need more than help with their immediate problems; they need an education in independence, so that eventually they will be able to live happily with their own unaided decisions.

Nearly all authorities agree that guidance should be seen as a continuous process, starting at least at the beginning of secondary school education, carrying through to the end of school and preferably followed up later on. Some hints about how such a scheme might develop have been provided by research, notably by Donald Super (1959), which has done much to establish the older view that vocational maturity was reached gradually, as the individual progressed through a number of stages of vocational growth. Super has suggested that between the ages of fourteen and eighteen years, or thereabouts, teenagers pass through a *tentative* stage, in which they develop a recognition of responsibility for choosing their careers and tentatively look at various careers in relation to themselves. This is followed by a *transitional* stage, in which the adolescent begins to equip himself with the necessary skills in his chosen area, and then the *establishment* stage is reached, in which the young adult obtains the necessary social recognition of his competence in a chosen area. Not all adolescents reach these stages at the same age, some appearing to mature vocationally faster than others.

Super's evidence is drawn from North America, but has received some support from research studies in the United Kingdom; for example by S.M. Chown's study (1958) of the formation of occupational choice among grammar school pupils from urban communities in England. Most people would probably agree with the general idea that children pass gradually from an infantile view of careers towards an adult appreciation in keeping with the evolution of their personalities from childhood towards maturity.

As a continuous process Vocational guidance cannot be separated from personal guidance. This is partly because the major decisions made during adolescence affect the individual's entire life, and not just its vocational aspects, and partly because the ability to reach vocational decisions is affected by the teenager's background as a whole. This has been found for example in America, where as we shall see in Chapter 6, guidance started as vocational guidance and gradually widened its scope to include personal guidance when it was found impossible to separate one from the other. While this truth is generally recognised in Britain in the few centres of higher education which run specialist courses in guidance, it is not so among teachers as a whole. Very occasionally someone who has worked in school guidance and realizes the need to integrate the vocational, educational, and personal development of pupils, publishes his findings, but such papers by teachers are unfortunately rare in everywhere at present.

To sum up the discussion so far by saying that guidance could be thought of as having three possible levels: single - stage guidance, which here means giving careers advice to the adolescent about to leave school, in the hope of easing problems which have already been allowed to mature'. (an example of what might be called *crisis counselling);* two - stage guidance, in which an attempt is made to reduce the size of the final problem of transition from school to work by combining educational with vocational guidance; and finally continuous guidance, in which the aim is to prevent major problems from developing as such, and to speed a maturity of outlook in the individual about his own life and its meaning. At this level it becomes impossible to separate vocational guidance from the wider process of personal guidance of which it forms part.

Due to various forms of guidance are so interwoven, that there is such a need today to build up teams containing people with different viewpoints, including parents, teachers, Youth Employment Officers, psychologists, social workers and medical doctors. But the: practical problems in organising such teams have not yet been resolved. The professions concerned have evolved within the boundaries of their own history, and their contact with each other is often tenuous. As a result, many parents and teachers have only a patchy knowledge of what services are available. In the following pages we shall hope to throw some light on this confused scene, as well as dealing with the question of organising guidance teams.

Vocational guidance in association with other forms of guidance has had a long history in American schools. Further, much of this experience has been gained in high schools of an essentially comprehensive nature, and is thus of particular interest to us as we develop our own comprehensive schools. The number of American publications on every aspect of guidance is prodigious in contrast to our own comparatively scanty published material. In a Jew years' time we may well have made good much of this difference, but at the present time there are, for example, no British handbooks on guidance techniques comparable to the work of Ruth Strang or L. Tyler; no books dealing with historical and philosophical issues in guidance comparable to the work of Wrenn, Beck, C.H. Miller, or E.G. Williamson, and no symposium comparable in range and depth to McGowan and Schmidt's *Counselling: Readings in Theory and Practice* (1962). Because these works are written in English, they are read widely in this country by scholars and workers who cannot yet obtain equivalent British material. The Schools Council Report on Counselling in Schools (1967), drew attention to the current strength of North American ideas in Britain, pointing out that both Keele and Reading universities had called on distinguished American theorists and practitioners in initiating their courses. The Report suggested that the influence stemmed from the length of experience which the Americans had gained in this field, and to the internal consistency of its theory, in contrast to the situation in Britain. Further, although there are differences in the cultural patterns of Britain and North America, many questions in guidance are shared in common, ranging from problems about techniques such as permissive and directive approaches to deeper issues about the relationship between the individual and the State. We are not suggesting that guidance in India should or will follow the pattern of North America, but that the present position gives us the opportunity to draw on the experience of a nation whose educational tradition is mainly derived from Europe, to adapt any techniques which may seem appropriate for our own uses, and possibly to avoid their mistakes.

The field of guidance in other European countries is also extremely interesting, but at present the pattern is changing so fast that a separate chapter would probably be dangerously out of date in a fairly short time. It is a pity that very little Continental work on guidance is available in English. The use of psychometric techniques may however often be very helpful at some stage in guidance, and the general public, including many teachers, still hold prejudices about such techniques, which in turn may lead them to prejudiced conclusions about the value of a system which makes use of them. Also many private firms, claiming to specialise in vocational guidance, now advertise services which rely heavily on psychometric procedures. The rapid spread of such organisations makes it important for people interested in guidance to have some knowledge of the values and limitations of these techniques.

'What is life like?' Three different levels of answer are possible: the levels of fact, of value, and of ultimate significance.

# 7

# Mental Hygiene and Guidance

"We work day after day, not to finish things; but to make the future better... becuase we will spend the rest of our lives there."

—*Charles F. Kettering*

No life can be complete with inadequate attitudes. Yet even a proper job and wholesome attitudes cannot make a satisfying design for living. The emotional starvation of large numbers of children and adults represents a greater problem than does the physical malnutrition of which so much is heard. The psychologist who meets these emotionally starved individuals when they have reached such a state as to become problems in mental hygiene can readily point out for the counselor certain evidences of such starvation.

**(1) Loneliness**

One evidence of such emotional non-equilibrium is loneliness. This inner emptiness of life is felt by all humankind at times. For sonic, these times are rare; for most, they are more frequent than is ever admitted; and for others, this loneliness is so real as to create the dominant problem in their lives. The needs of those in this last category will be chiefly considered here, but methods which are effective for the last group can, to a greater or lesser degree, be used in meeting' the problems caused by loneliness in whatever sphere it may be found.

Loneliness appears in many guises, only one of which will be discussed here. For example, it often happens that those who are most lonely give the least impression of it. *The eyes of the counselor must be keen, indeed, to detect as symptoms of loneliness an extratense, over-intense, highly-keyed demonstration of gaiety by the counselor.* This overcompensating individual may be characterised as the "life of the party." These individuals frequently give of themselves to the utmost in the hope that they can thus keep others from being as lonely as they are. Frequently, also, by putting on such a show, it is possible for them to forget the ache of their own lives for a little while. Generally, happiness is quiet in its manifestations. The individual whose emotions are poised often leads the fun without being the "life of the party." Emotional poise comes to the individual who feels that his emotional investment in life are returned with interest, and 'who feels secure in his life relationships. If the "life of the party" could be seen alone one hour after the party, a misty eye which held back a tear, a look of having fought for something which wasn't there, is far more apt to characterize the face than the broad smile of the party hours. There is a tragedy about these lives which may follow them throughout Friends of these typical "life-of-the-party" individuals feel that they are self-sufficient and never lonely or afraid hence, these friends bring only their laughter and lighter moments to the "life of the party."

Never to have had a friend care enough to share a burden is never to have had a friend; and never to have had a friend with whom one felt free to share is to have lived a very lonely life. Human, beings don't share burdens with those whom they feel have never carried them. The counselor is wise who remembers in conferences with the individual student that the gay front with which that student faces the world is no guarantee of a gay spirit when that same student shuts the world out and sits alone when evening comes. Loneliness is essentially a state of psychic incompleteness, a state of tension which can be most effectively relieved by satisfying companionship. The guidance worker must always realize that there may be, and probably is, before him an individual who is lonely for the companionship of someone with whom a "oneness" is felt—someone with whom he shares, and who shares with him, that side of life which the world never sees.

A feverish activity of any type on the part of an individual is almost as valid as a yellow caution signal saying, "Loneliness here." In school these students are apt to try to be in too many activities. Their unexpressed motto seems to be, "Let me do everything, anything, so that I may not have to face the loneliness that is in me." Some of the finest people in student life are found in this category. These individuals lead uncentered lives. A futility overtone dominates their philosophy. Their need is for a sense of psychic unity with someone. That someone may be any individual with whom a sense of "oneness" can be established. The "breath of life" in a very real sense is just this common spiritual breathing with a friend—this sharing of the whole of daily living, not only life's happiness and triumph, but also its sadness and disappointment. Just as some blood types call for certain other blood types, and only certain blood types, before an effective transfusion and then adequate fusion can occur, even so it seems that some personalities require certain other personalities, and only certain other personalities, for the true fusion of friendship to be reached.

The counselor's tasks is not to find the necessary friend for the individual, but instead to point the way toward friendship. Contrary to many popular approaches to human relationships, the student may be led to see that the real friends, those very few (any individual is fortunate who has one such friend) with whom a sense of psychic unity is established, are never won in mass. Such a friend is too vital for a full life for the student to leave to chance his ever having such a friendship. It should be pointed out to the student that this friend may be someone of the same or opposite sex, the same age or any different age, related or not related; but that when he finds this friend he will know it, for both of them will share, and life will no longer be lonely for either. The counselor should stress the fact that the finding of such a friend is the easiest part of such a relationship, that if something beautiful is to be built in the way of a continuing sense of oneness, *both must share unreservedly all of those phases of their lives which can in any way affect one another.* Further, as an aid to the student's own philosophy of friendship, the counselor may develop some such thoughts on the following: In every human being there is some virtue worthy of the respect, the admiration, and the belief of a friend. Every human being needs to know that someone believes in him. Friendship lifts us from what we are into what we may become. We try to measure up to the vision of someone who has faith in us. It is the part of a friend to hold fast to his faith in the best his friend can become. The power for progressive living is thus developed from vital human relationships. Few cases, indeed, would ever need the therapeutic aid of the mental hygienist if, through high school and on, every individual faced life secure in the relationship of a strong psychic unity with someone. It is the counselor's part, first, to recognize the loneliness of these individuals who have not attained such relationships; second, to show them how to be and to hold friends; and third, to give to each individual a philosophy of friendship which will help him, when once a friend is found, to seek to understand rather than to change, to believe always the best and to be loyal.

Basic physiological trends, psychological predispositions, or other factors such as fame, fortune, beauty, and power cannot form a sufficient barrier to keep loneliness away. It is most apt to be found with the most favoured; those who walk the peaks of life are those who walk alone. The masses may bow in homage, but those who could be friends stay away because they feel they are not needed. Particularly with brilliant students the counselor should be on the watch for loneliness. Its symptoms vary with the individual and with different individuals at different times. Though some of the most glaring symptoms can readily be recognized, it is very probably true that the counselor must have a sense of "oneness" with the individual being counseled before the signals of loneliness which most individuals try to hide can be discerned.

The wide-awake counselor who is always on the watch for such symptoms will probably find them far more frequently than he expects. The lives most people live behind their faces are lonely lives. Civilisation has brought much of comfort, but human beings at this stage of our culture are afraid of the happiness they can bring to one another. Some are so afraid of the pain which comes when a psychic tie is broken that they lack the courage ever to establish such a tie. Much stress is being placed on loneliness as a contributory cause to emotional starvation because there is so much of loneliness. Much stress is being placed on the type of human relationship which will banish this loneliness, because such relationships are rare. Yet for every human being who is capable of loneliness, and exactly to the extent that he is capable of being lonely, there is the possibility of realising this satisfying relationship. The courageous spirits who have attained great friendships have recognised that they come only through sacrifice, that there is no such thing as their springing into full bloom and continuing to be a real vital force without much of self-giving I and sharing on the part of both individuals.

To those who are lonely, and that means to most human beings, the counselor has given a great gift if he inspires them to go and find a real friend, and then to be one.

**(2) Insecurity**

Insecurity is the second factor basic to much emotional starvation. When the counselor comes to deal with the insecure student, a bit of introspection is in order. The counselor is more humble and more able to meet the student's need if he looks within his own life and remembers how he felt when he first faced that baffling problem of inadequate expression which is at the core of insecurity. It is important that the counselor be able to approach every counseling situation with the spirit of a helper, and not with that of a master. Especially is this true when the counseling situation involves an insecure individual. Edward Carpenter recognised the need for such counselor humility when he wrote:

> Who are you who go about to save them that are lost?
>
> Are you saved yourself?
>
> Do you know that who would save his own life must lose it?
>
> Are you then one of the lost?
>
> Be sure, very sure, that each of these can teach you as much as,
>
> Probably more than, you can teach them.
>
> Have you sat humbly at their feet, and waited on their lips that they
>
> Should be the first to speak—and been reverent before these
>
> children Whom you so little understand?
>
> Have you dropped into the bottomless pit from between yourself and them
>
> All hallucination of superiority, all flatulence of knowledge, and
>
> Every shred of abhorrence and loathing?
>
> Is it equal, is it free as the wind between you?

Could you be happy receiving favours from one of the most despised of these?

Could you yourself be one of the lost?

Arise, then, and become a Saviour.

If there is an individual who has never known a sense of insecurity, let that individual seek his life's work elsewhere than in the counselor's seat. One criterion for maturity is the capacity to suffer, and one of humankind's most common sufferings is an "emotional state of not being sure."

It is the mature individual who knows how to *remember* who should sit on the counselor's side of the desk and give advice.

Very few individuals will say to a counselor, "I brings to you this my problem of insecurity." It is the counselor who must see what the basic problem really is, while the individual talks of troublesome surface matters which are the outgrowth of more basic causes. The counselor's eyes must be very keen and very alert for symptoms of insecurity. These symptoms are of many kinds. For example, physical expressions of insecurity are evidenced frequently by the individual who can't find just where to put his hands, whose throat seems constantly to need to be cleared, whose color changes easily with no apparent reason—indeed, the individual whose nervous reactions are such as to focus the attention of those who are with him upon his person rather than upon his thinking.

Imagination and kindness are the greatest needs of the counselor when he is dealing with individuals dominated by a sense of insecurity. Here, kindness can very well be born of a memory of having also suffered; for if one has lived intently and with courage and vision, there is almost surely the very real memory of the day when hands seemed made to sit on, and the chief reason for having feet seemed to be to find a place to hide them—the day when one wasn't if able to find quite the fitting words as adequate vehicles for thoughts. The counselor's imagination might well have as its basis a knowledge of the broad psychological causes of insecurity plus a store of tact laid by through years of experience in dealing with humankind and their problems

Many individuals feel insecure because of *improper grooming*. We sometimes find here the boy whose legs have outgrown his pants, and whose arms have outgrown his sleeves. For example, a boy who was giving definite trouble as an *attention-getter* in his classes was found by one of the authors to be wearing shirts he had outgrown. His school history until this time had been exemplary; his I.Q. was 150. Investigation showed that he was being raised by an aunt with very rigid ideas about economy. She had sent the boy to town to buy some shirts the summer before. The boy had found a shirt bargain sale, and hoping to please her had bought twelve shirts at once. The shirts were not returnable. The aunt failed to see the boy's attempt at economy by buying bargain shirts in quantity; instead, she saw the extravagance of buying more shirts than necessary. Therefore, in order to teach him a lesson, she had decreed that he must wear the shirts until he had worn them out—regardless of whether or not he had outgrown them. Four inches of his bare arm extended below the shirt cuff had proved too much for classmates at an age when teasing is one of the reasons for living, and Joe's classmates hadn't spared him. In fact, because he made better grades than any of them, they teased him with added zeal. The result was an effort on Joe's part to compensate for the felt physical insecurity by seeking attention in every other possible way. Now Joe's father was a *very* able professional man. The difficulty was explained to the father in confidence and without Joe's knowledge. The week following the conference with the father, Joe came to school wearing shirts that fitted him.

All insecurity problems arising from socially inadequate clothing are not so readily solved. Frequently the individual in question is wearing hand-me-downs and has little or no money with which to buy other clothes. In such instances, conferences on making the most out of the clothes one has can be very helpful. Once the counselor has sufficiently got the confidence of the student so that the problem can be faced, much can be done in the way of sound advice as to color combinations, possible alterations, frequent home washings and pressings, and, perhaps, in some instances a freshening by tinting. It is good technique for the individuals trying to face socially inadequate clothing problems to report to the counselor regularly for a period of a month or so for recommendations and suggestions. In this way, the counselor can note the actual results of the counseling which has gone before.

Improper grooming which is due to carelessness and indifference should, of course, be dealt with in a very different and in a very factual manner. The counselor should, however, make very sure that a seeming attitude of carelessness or indifference is not a mask for lack of funds for clothes or lack of knowledge about what to wear and when to wear it. If, however, no lack of funds exists, and adequate knowledge regarding what to wear and when to wear it is found to be one of the individual's assets, the counselor is confronted with a problem which may have such deep psychological implications that a psychologist should be brought into the case.

The counselor's first question may be, "What motives are basic to this individual's emotional life?" Unless the breakdown of the motives which underlie these emotional strivings is complete and is faced, carelessness and indifference is apt to manifest itself, not only in clothing, but also in speech, cleanliness, manners, and habits of all kinds, studious and otherwise. Hence, the counselor's problem is to study such an individual with reference to his emotional background. If, after a careful examination, the counselor finds no excuse for the manifest carelessness and indifference, the services of a trained psychologist should immediately be enlisted. However, many "clothing-indifference" problems can be handled effectively by the counselor.

**(3) Bodily Defects**

*Bodily defects* upon which the individual is placing too much emphasis give rise to another source of physical insecurity. These defects may range all the way from pimples on the adolescent's face to a hunchback or a harelip; from a small birthmark on the forehead to a short leg or paralysed arm. These defects may, indeed, be any physical handicap over which the individual has no known control. Inasmuch as these conditions are permanent, the feelings of insecurity occasioned by them readily give way to attitudes of inferiority. No attempt is made here to summarize all the factors in life which may give rise to feelings of physical insecurity. The emphasis here is upon the need for seeking the cause of the insecurity and for helping the individual to help himself so completely that poise and personal control become dominant in that area of his life which was formerly characterised by a sense of insecurity.

**(4) Inadequate Social Knowledge**

The great prevalence of social insecurity even among adults is amply attested to by the large sale of books which deal with proper social usage. A helpful part of every alert counselor's programme is some type of "manners club" in which proper etiquette and correct social form are both studied and practiced. Most counselors are familiar with the girl who is socially insecure—who doesn't know when to stand up to acknowledge an introduction, when and how to take a boy's arm, or what to do at a dance when she finds herself alone—and with the boy who isn't quite sure of the proper form for introducing his new girl to his old friends, who doesn't know how to address a gentleman older than himself. When inadequate social knowledge is causing embarrassment and consequent insecurity, the counselor's remedy is plainly adequate social knowledge. One of the least painful ways of obtaining this knowledge is through some type of manners club. However, if such a club is to be a success, the counselor must be very careful in the organisational approach to make sure that there is some type of social approval placed upon obtaining membership in the club. In other words, such a club is doomed to failure before it is begun if those who are members are thought to obtain membership because they have no manners or social graces. One counselor whose manners club was quite the proper high-school club made membership obtainable only when some special school service had been performed which was considered by the counselor, the dean, and one teacher to have sufficient worth to merit for the performer a membership in the club. In this way the counselor was able to give the individual security by giving him a school task of responsibility which he was able to do with satisfaction to himself, and, also, those individuals who gave evidence of needing such a club were thus indirectly guided to it.

Social insecurity is caused by many factors other than lack of social knowledge and training. It may be that racial distinction, occupational family background, homes on the wrong side of the tracks, divorced parents, parents in jail or otherwise without social approval, or perhaps a knowledge of illegitimacy is contributing to a person's continued sense of social insecurity. For these cases the counselor needs to give the individual a broader sense of life's values. There is here a definite need for a reading course which will contribute toward a reorientation of personal values. The counselor needs at hand a list of books so classified that as soon as the problem is recognized, the individual may be guided to the proper reading material.

Nor does the counselor's task end with having given a reading-material suggestion. The counselor-teacher relationship then comes into play, perhaps in this manner. The teacher may be sent a note suggesting that the student would like to make his next "book report" on the book the counselor has suggested, or the public-speaking teacher may co-operate with the counselor by asking the boy to make a speech on the subject material contained in the book. The avenues for such co-operation are legion. The counselor's second step, however, is definite: a follow-up conference to make sure that the new and suggested values have become an active part of the individual's daily motivation; and, hence, that the social insecurity caused by the displaced value is no more.

**(5) Emotional Insecurity**

*Emotional insecurity,* as interpreted here, refers only to those feelings of insecurity which have an emotional origin. The individual who is a stranger in a group and is not sure of being either wanted or accepted; the person who is dominated by the fear that he will not be liked by his fellows and who, therefore, feels conscious of himself and socially out of place when in a group; the individual who is always afraid of saying or doing the wrong thing-such individuals are emotionally insecure. Such feelings of insecurity have flowered many a party wall, and have caused tears to soak many a pillow after the party.

The psychologically trained counselor in seeking the causes of insecurity during the adolescent period should remember, while emotion is present throughout life, it is frequently strongest in its manifestations during the turbulent period of adolescence. Emotion may be exhibited in any number of types of responses or in any combination of such responses. In terms of current psychological research, *emotion* manifests itself chiefly in adient or avoidance responses or in some degree of combination of the two. For example, love is considered as an adient response, fear and anger as avoidance responses. The teacher or counselor, then, recognising the strong current of emotion, can hold broadly that many emotional states are derived directly from the emotional responses of *love, fear,* and *anger,* or from some combination thereof, and that emotional insecurity is almost always based upon uncertainty regarding proper outlets for the physiological tensions basic to these dominant emotions. For example, the counselor may find himself confronted with an individual whose emotional insecurity springs from a repressed or otherwise unexpressed love emotion or, perhaps, from an unrequited love. It is possibly one of life's most desolate moments when the fact must be faced that one loves someone who doesn't love in return. Grave doubts as to one's own worth are at once engendered. These doubts spread throughout the whole of the individual's life relationships. A general state of emotional insecurity results. Physiologically this state is, perhaps, best described as one of unrelieved tension, the extent of the emotion being determined by the intensity of the tension. Whether the counselor gives advice to the lovelorn, or shows the individual how to effect an emotional transfer either to creative work or to some more responsive individual, depends entirely on the case.

Such problems are so very frequent at the secondary-school level that the account of an experience of one of the authors may be helpful.

Emotional insecurity may just as easily be based on fear which the individual doesn't know how to face. For example, it is not uncommon for adolescents to have doubts regarding their parentage, or to be concerned lest they have cancer or some other hidden and malignant disease. Also, success has been heralded with such fervor by parents, teachers, friends, and leaders that one of the most frequently met fears is the fear of failure. Success has been talked about so much more than failure that the adolescent who finds even a normal percentage of failure in his life sometimes conies to believe himself worthless. Little does he realize that father at the dinner table tells only the success stories of his day, and that mother really does remember only the success stories of her adolescent years.

So much talk of success makes the adolescent feel unique as he honestly faces the fact that his life has more of failure in it than of success. Perhaps he worked for and hoped for the position of captain of the baseball team and in the final line-up found himself a substitute catcher. Perhaps he wanted to be president of the high-school debating team and actually found himself with no office and with the insignificant post of alternate speaker on the negative side of a question when his beliefs were entirely in sympathy with the affirmative. Perhaps he were his best Sunday blue serge suit with the long, grown-up trousers to school in the hope of getting a certain girl to consent to go to the high-school dance with him, only to find that she was going with a boy whom he very much disliked.

Teachers, parents, adolescent leaders, somehow fail to emphasize as much the many things they have dreamed about and worked for that never happened as they emphasize those few occasions in their lives when they have had the mountain-top experience of being able to say, "I wanted this, I worked for it, and I got it. I have succeeded." This problem is by no means isolated or simple. Youth is being cheated out of much of happiness and self-understanding through the "I-am-a-success" declaring habit of those to whom he turns for leadership. Consequently, the youth often enters the tasks of his life with the profound belief that he fails more frequently than does anyone else. Unless he is very sound emotionally, he is even likely to come to feel sorry for himself and thus start the groundwork for an ineffectual life. He needs to see the uncolored facts of success and failure as they actually are in the lives of those he admires and strives to be like unto.

Continued experience of emotional insecurity based on fear readily leads to the habit of fear. The habit of being afraid has caused many individuals to go to the mental hygienist who would never have gone had the habit of fearlessness been acquired instead. One tragedy of these fear-filled lives is that this habit is sometimes inspired by the too great caution of a devoted parent. Once the habit of fear is acquired, it grows and spreads like a parasitic vine through the many and various life reactions of the individual. To be afraid one can't is the first step toward believing one can't, and believing one can't is the first step toward not being able to.

The counselor will meet this primal emotion of fear in many, many forms. One student will confess he is afraid of failing his algebra; another that he is afraid he won't make his track letter; and another that she is afraid her boy friend loves another girl; and perhaps a fourth that she is afraid she will never be attractive. Whenever and where-ever fear presents itself, the guide's part is to inspire self-confidence. Fear grows like a gnawing pain, and rapidly; but self-confidence based on individual achievement worthy of that confidence grows even more rapidly, and as a positive force gradually wipes out the negative force of fear. The counselor should be led to try first those things in which success is probable, and then gradually, as his confidence grows, tasks in which success is less sure. He should be taught to recognize that a step is made toward emotional adulthood when there is meaning for him in the statement that "All endeavor involves the risk of failure as well as the possibility of success."

Any situation for which the individual has no adequate patterns of reaction is likely to be a fear-producing situation.

There is no fear known to man which may not be dominating the adolescent and causing within him a high degree of emotional insecurity. Fear is an elemental emotion. The alert counselor is ever on the watch for its manifestation.

Anger, perhaps arising from a general feeling of injustice, frequently leads the adolescent, or any individual for that matter, into a state of emotional insecurity.

Individuals whose almost certain reactions to life's situations are negative ones; individuals who are not able to accept at face value the faith and love which comes into their lives because they can't help feeling that there must be a catch somewhere; individuals who are quick to show indifference, quick to hurt someone who loves them Jest the one who loves them should get to be the first to be indifferent or to hurt—these individuals frequently have suffered from some actual injustice somewhere in their lives, some injustice which hurt them so deeply as to color their entire life reactions. Such persons are often twelve-cylinder people in native endowment and one-cylinder persons in life expression. A part of the counselor's job is to find them and to help them before it is too late.

The three emotional horsemen of the apocalypse are certainly unfulfilled love, fear, and anger, or some combination of these. Physiologically and psychologically these foes of emotional well-being and healthful living depress and incapacitate the individual. If these states are not recognised and dealt with, an emotionally insecure and hence handicapped individual is an almost certain result. All the handicapped are not on crutches; many of them live under the shadow of the fear in their hearts; not all of them are blind, for many of them with anger see life only through the blackness of some early injustice. Indeed, all of the handicapped are not the deaf and dumb, for many of them carry the sorrow of loving but not being loved, with the attendant depressing conviction that as individuals they are so inferior that no one can love them. In any of these states the counselor's technique is to find the primary emotion which is failing to find adequate expression, and then, as far as possible, to lead the individual, first, to understand the cause of his own insecurity, and then to take positive steps to remedy it.

**(6) Mental Insecurity**

A form of insecurity which is rather infrequently encountered is mental insecurity. Perhaps the reason for the infrequency is that good minds are scarce, and generally the self-critical minds are the good minds. Morons make with dogmatic certainty statements that would cause the genius to ponder long. Frequently, because of thorough thinking processes, possessors of good minds remain silent while glib lesser minds influence the day. However, the evaluation of the multitude often becomes the evaluation that these individuals accept for themselves if thus far in life their mental efforts have brought them little of the fruits of success. After a few occasions of seeing the smooth-of-tongue gain the day, these individuals are very likely to feel not too certain of their own merits and accept the status given them by the multitude. Such is the entrance to the road which leads a good mind to become *a timid soul.* When these timid minds do gather courage to express themselves, they often recognize the many qualifications necessary for any factual statement to be made, and are likely to speak with such *uncertainty* that those who hear catch only the doubt and not the thought. Soon these individuals conic to feel the need of supporting authority from other minds. Instead of bodily speaking out in the dignity of their own right as breathing, effecting, and thinking human beings, they cast about for the thoughts of someone else which are similar to their own in the hope that the authority of an accepted name will win acceptance for the thought contribution. And thus, instead of walking fearlessly and alone, they begin to walk fearfully and on mental crutches.

Unless these individuals are found and guided adequately in school, their sense of mental insecurity will very probably relegate their good minds to places of mediocrity in life. They suffer from too great respect for others and from too little respect for themselves. The wise counselor who knows the intelligence scores of those who are counseled will be on guard for this type of insecurity among brilliant students. When it is found, the counselor must lead the student to see the difficulty within himself and then to recognize his own value. These individuals are among the few who are sometimes benefited by knowing their I.Q. scores. The authors have also found that guidance toward the art of self-expression is helpful in such cases of mental insecurity. Mental insecurity caused by real inferiority is sometimes found in the too bold and often exponentially limited individuals who make statements for *effect,* in the overly dramatic persons whose distrust of the validity of their own knowledge is such that they seek to hold the center of attention by an overpowering emotional appeal.

**(7) Economic Insecurity**

During recent depression years economic insecurity has come to be a chronic social ailment. Many counselors who deal with economic insecurity feel that they are performing a socially useful service when they teach the individual to place his values elsewhere than in the economic sphere. Such a service is not enough. The primal needs requisite to survival are involved. The individual feels that he has asked for bread and been given a stone when he has asked for a path to lead him toward economic security and has been told that he should place his values elsewhere—that many phases of life are of more importance than its economic phases. Quite rightly, the individual gives first place to the impelling thought, "I want to know I can cat tomorrow and sleep tonight." This acute economic need is not generally met until the youth has finished secondary school, but economic insecurity frequently is felt intensely by the secondary-school student because of his home situation and because of the responsibilities which he knows he must face as soon as his secondary schooling is over.

The wise counselor doesn't try to paint a rose-colored picture, nor is there any endeavor to brush away the youth's fears; instead, the energy which is going into the production of fear is directed toward constructive channels. The youth is given, as nearly as the counselor is able to give it, a factual picture of the economic situation. His enthusiasm and imagination are enlisted in an effort to work wholeheartedly with the counselor in an endeavor to determine in what way his own peculiar and particular abilities can most effectively be utilised in this current, not too inviting, economic order.

Thus, in a very healthy and positive manner, the youth is led to work harder and more purposefully toward a life goal which includes an occupational area for which his capacities lit him. It is the guidance worker's aim to see to it that the student loses his sense of economic insecurity in a constructive urge to develop fully his own potentialities, ever cognizant of the fact that life gives no guarantees, but that the race is frequently for the one who is prepared, for the one who knows his strength and how, and when, and where to use it.

**Conclusion**

Loneliness and insecurity are two great contributors toward emotional starvation. The counselor who helps students to meet and defeat these two heralds of misery' has functioned effectively in one very important sphere of counseling opportunities.

## *REFERENCES*

Carpenter Edward , *Towards Democracy* (A. and C. Boni, New York, 1955) as quoted by Elliot and Klliot, *Solving Personal Problems,* Henry Holt and Co., New York, 1936, p. 196.

Elliot and Elliot, *Solving Personal Problems,* Henry Holt and Co., New York, 1936, p. 32.

# 8

# Guidance Services

Guidance, which is most crucial in the modern school system in particular, needs a proper planning and establishment. Careers teachers form only one of many groups who help guide young people, including churches, political bodies and various charitable organisations which could rightly claim a place here.

### Youth Employment Service

*(a) History*

At the beginning of the last century there were only a few voluntary bodies which offered information about work, but in 1909 the first national provision appeared, when juvenile departments were attached to some Employment Exchanges to help place boys and girls in jobs. An Act of the following year allowed Local Education Authorities a somewhat similar function, so that from the start there sprang up a system of dual control—Employment Exchanges on the one hand, Local Education Authorities on the other. Although an agreement was soon reached for guidance to be undertaken by the local authorities, and placement by the Employment Exchanges, there was a good deal of overlapping of effort. This increased in 1920 when unemployment insurance was extended to boys and girls aged sixteen. So in 1923 L.E.A.S were given the choice of running their own juvenile employment sendee, or leaving it to the Ministry of Labour. In 1927 central control of the Service was vested in this Ministry. Thereafter nothing else of great importance happened until the Ince Report, 1945, recommended that a Central Youth Employment Executive (C.Y.E.E.) should be set up to advise the Ministry on the future running of the Service, and that it should be staffed by representatives of the Ministry, the Department of Education and Science (as it is now called), and the Scottish Education Department. It was also suggested that all L.E.A.S should make a final decision about running their own Employment Service, or leave all work in their area to the Ministry of Labour. This became law through the subsequent Employment and Training Act of 1948, from which the name Youth Employment Service dates. A National Youth Employment Council was appointed to advise the C.Y.E.E., and L.E.A.S were given six months' grace for their decision, during which about 71% accepted responsibility for organizing their own Service.

*(b) Functions of the Youth Employment Service*

The traditional functions, still accepted today, are these:

1. To give young people up-to-date information about jobs and careers.
2. To give vocational guidance to boys and girls at school in their later years, and after they have left, up to the age of eighteen years.
3. To help boys and girls find suitable work, and to help employers find suitable workers.
4. To follow up the progress of young people in their jobs, and to give them whatever other help they need.

As well as this, the Service administers National Insurance and Assistance, wherever they apply to young workers.

The success of the Service in providing comprehensive vocational guidance and placement is greatly limited by the heavy case load of its officers. In April 1964, these amounted to between 400 and 600 persons per officer in the L.E.A. areas; in 1965, according to the Albemarle Report, the national average Was 533 per officer. Pressure of this sort has reduced the work in schools sometimes to one talk per annum, given by the officer to a class of leavers, and one short interview with each pupil in his final year.

The advice is too little and too late; pupils are often inadequately prepared beforehand. Under such circumstances the officer meets a barrier of ignorance and apathy on the part of many early leavers, against which he can do very little without a full knowledge of the child's aptitudes, interests, and home background. Where pupils have been prepared beforehand even the minimum of one talk and one interview can do some good. Much thus depends on the relationships between school staff and Youth Employment Officers, as recognized in the Albemarle Report.

*(c) The Training of Youth Employment Officers*

Although not all Youth Employment Officers are trained, courses have existed since 1948, when the first one started at Lamorbey Park in Sideup. The Piercy Report of 1951 emphasized the need for a good quality of applicants, and for a minimum of one year's preliminary training for officers. Unfortunately Britain was deep in one of her post-war economic troubles when the Report came out, and the only recommendation adopted was that which urged the provision of short courses for existing untrained officers. These, varying in length from five days to six months, appeared during the following years, the longer ones usually being held at Lamorbey Park and at Birkbeck College, London. The only Officers to receive a year's training were those lucky enough to attend the full course at Lamorbey Park, a small fraction of the total. The inadequacy of training facilities was pointed out in the Savage Report, published in 1960, which led to the founding of a Youth Employment Training Board in 1961, to keep the needs of the Service under review. As a result of this, a new annual training course on lines similar to those of the Lamorbey Park course was started in the following year at Manchester Chamber College of Commerce. The Training Board also co-ordinates publicity for the Service, acts as a clearing house for admissions, aids in selection, and promotes short courses for serving officers. At present training facilities allow all Ministry officers to have three months' intermittent instruction during the first year of their service.

*(d) The Albemarle Report*

This document was prepared by a working part of the National Youth Employment Council, briefed to define the issues facing the Service in the light of recent developments in education, and the changing needs of industry. Its main findings were:

1. Ministry Youth Employment Officers require only the three months' training provided at present.
2. All Local Education Authority Youth Employment Officers should receive one year's training before entry, after a given date.
3. More short courses should be provided for existing officers.
4. The system of dual control between the Ministry and the Local Education Authorities is a mutual stimulus, and should remain.
5. Officers should extend their school vocational guidance work downwards to include years earlier than the last school year; upwards to help people older than eighteen, and outwards to include further education establishments and parents.
6. Placement of pupils in jobs is properly the work of the Youth Employment Service and not of the schools.

7. Links with employers should be strengthened, and a deeper study of job requirements should be made: follow-up of young workers should be extended; and the Service should generally extend its liaison functions as a link between education and industry.
8. The Central Youth Employment Executive should co-ordinate more research into the Youth Employment field.
9. To meet these requirements, staff increases are needed; rational salary scales for posts of comparable responsibility should be introduced, and where the Ministry provides the Service, a senior tier of experienced officers should be posted.

The Albemarle Report makes a few good points, including the need for closer liaison with schools, parents, and the world of work as well as for more thorough training of officers. The identity of educational and vocational guidance is recognized in suggestions that the Youth Employment Officer should follow a pupil's progress right through school and the transition to work.

But in many ways the Report makes sad reading. Two years before its publication, Alec Rodger (1963) drew attention to the major weaknesses of the service. He pointed out that it was understaffed, and that the inadequate provision was due to lack of funds, arising in turn from public apathy which meant that politicians dared not risk the displeasure of their constituents by advocating expenditure where there was no great public demand. He attacked the system of dual control, suggesting that L.E.A. officers tended to be individual-orientated, and Ministry officers job-orientated. These and other possibilities seem to have been inadequately dealt with by the Report. In the Albemarle Report a major idea is to extend the services, whereas the staff/pupil ratio indicates that even present commitments strain it severely. This overriding difficulty is glossed over with some general remarks about the staff /pupil ratio being no longer an adequate measure of an officer's work; with some suggestions about providing employment assistants to take over routine work; and with an exhortation for staffing needs to be kept under review. It is even doubtful if a single year of training will be enough for an officer who is, among other things, to counsel parents as well as adolescents, to follow in greater depth than before the changing pattern of industry, and to undertake job analysis. The system of dual control is supported, whereas in the closely related field of English education its presence since 1870 has been a constant source of friction, as shown for example by H. C. Barnard's work, mentioned earlier. If implemented, the proposals in the Albemarle Report would create an even wider separation than now exists between officers in the service of the Ministry and those working for Local Education Authorities. Finally in a number of small points the Report is disturbing; for example in suggesting that pupils can assess their own 'strengths and weaknesses, likes and dislikes' (para. 46); and in the assumption that parents know the choice of a career to be a momentous step for a boy or girl to take unaided (para. 83), an assumption which seems to ignore the findings of sociological research referred to in earlier chapters, that many working class parents do not see initial employment in this light.

In spite of its shortcomings, the Youth Employment Service meets a need, shared by all modern western civilisations, to have a guidance organisation to cover the transition from school to work. Often the individual officer is a man or woman of high aptitude and determination whose enterprise surmounts many of the difficulties imposed by the system. The need seems to be for a closer examination of these difficulties, and of the position which the Service should hold in relation to other guidance organisations now rising into prominence with the growing importance of education.

**National Institute of Industrial Psychology**

Founded in 1921, this is a specialist vocational advice institute, independently controlled. By the use of a highly trained and expert body of guidance specialists, it aims to help young people to come to a clearer realisation of their aptitudes, attainments, interests, disposition and circumstances in the light of occupational demands. In other words, its experts give and interpret psychological tests to young people worried about their careers. Barnard has described it as a more ambitious method of vocational guidance than that of the Youth Employment Service, and its field is also rather more restricted, being mainly aimed at young people between the ages of sixteen and twenty-three years old, including late school leavers and undergraduates. The procedures used by the N.I.I.P. have been developed over many years of research, financed from funds provided by the Carnegie Trust, the Ministry of Technology, and by private members. A non-profit making body, it charges a fee of £25 per applicant (1969), and proceeds are used solely for the cost of giving advice.

Applications for guidance are received at the Institute's offices at 14 Welbeck Street, London W.I, and a questionnaire is sent out. This is completed by the client, or by the parent or guardian in the case of younger people. This provides he Institute with general data about the applicant's background, interests and career problems, and it is followed by an invitation to the first of two interviews at the Institute. Here, in groups of eight or ten, clients do a range of intelligence, aptitude and attainment tests, mainly of a pencil and paper kind, designed to provide the maximum of information without exposing people to strain. This is followed within ten days by a second visit, spent in an interview with a graduate psychologist, on the Institute's staff, and the completion of a few tests requiring individual supervision. Where parents agree, a confidential report is also obtained from the school principal of younger applicants, and the adviser likes to see the parents or guardian at the beginning and end of the second visit. All the evidence is then put together, and its vocational significance is discussed. Finally the psychologist prepares a report which summarizes the findings and suggests additional sources of information about suitable careers. Where necessary, the Institute will offer a further interview of up to one hour without extra charge, at a later date.

But attempts were made by the Institute to place clients in jobs, or to make investigations into the causes of educational backwardness, or to advise on choice of schools; but occasionally educational guidance on choosing school subjects is offered to candidates under the age of sixteen years. The Institute can also arrange to send a team to visit schools, and conduct tests and interviews on the premises, where six or more pupils wish to avail themselves of its aid. In these cases the fee is discussed between the Institute and the school concerned.

To assess the accuracy of its services, the Institute carries out follow-up studies; a questionnaire is sent out shortly after a careers decision is likely to have been made, and a second one from three to five years later. From a survey conducted on 250 such cases, N.I.I.P. claims 47% close agreement with the original prognosis, 23% fair agreement, and 17% poor agreement, the remainder providing insufficient data for a conclusion. Most of the 17% poor agreement was found among persons emotionally disturbed, under employed, or otherwise not using their abilities to best advantage (N.I.I.P. 1964). The Institute has also been engaged in the past on wider issues, such as experiments conducted with Local Education Authorities in Birmingham and Warrington in Unking its services with those of the Youth Employment Bureaux. The high consultation fees limit the extent of development along these lines, but it is a sign of the times that the waiting lists for individual consultations; are at present several months long.

**Other Specialists in Vocational Guidance**

Some of the post-graduate university courses mentioned earlier do a small amount of practical guidance with children. The Applied Psychology Unit of Edinburgh University, which trams honours psychology graduates in guidance, also does practical work which gives experience to students; in addition, it offers fully qualified professional advice on a fee-paying basis. The Careers Research and Advisory Centre at Cambridge answers questions on vocational guidance for a small charge.

Since the war a number of private firms specializing in vocational guidance have appeared. The more reputable of these usually advertise in such papers as *The Times* and the *Guardian*. Fees vary around ten guineas. For a lower price, appraisal tests can be sent through the post to clients. As these firms do not publish any data about the standardisation of their tests, it is impossible to assess their value.

**National Foundation for Educational Research**

This organisation was formally set up before the Second World War, when a special research fund, stemming from voluntary contributions, was organised and administered by London University Institute of Education. It emerged in 1945 as a national body, but its main work dates from 1947. As Ben Morris emphasized (1952), N.F.E.R. is essentially a post-war institution, paralleling the development of Institutes of Education, and attempts by the teaching profession to increase its range of professional skills. The influence of the Foundation on guidance is indirect but important. It concentrates on applied research in education, such as making and designing standardized tests for use in schools, and carrying out intensive research studies. Details of these are published each year in the N.F.E.R. *Annual Report.* The

Foundation has recently begun research into the development and evaluation of guidance systems in secondary education. Its objectives are to find out from teachers of adolescents what the teachers regard as the most urgent needs for increasing the effectiveness of guidance; to appraise existing instruments relevant for guidance; and to examine problems of guidance in the transition of pupils between secondary schools and institutes of further education. N.F.E.R. hopes that this research will lead to the development of test instruments, questionnaires, and other devices for use in guidance; to the development of guidance systems in schools; and to an evaluation of their effectiveness. It expects to do follow-up studies to see if the work helps pupils in making satisfactory educational and vocational decisions in later life Examples of other researches relevant for guidance are a long-term enquiry into problems in the transition from primary to secondary education; a study of factors in the organisation and life of secondary schools which affect the performance, attitudes and behaviour of pupils; a study of the extent to which career choices in technology are influenced by secondary technical school environment; and an earlier one into the use of school records of individual pupils. The findings of research studies are published regularly, along with other N.F.E.R. publications, details of which can be obtained by writing to the Foundation's offices.

**School Psychological Service**

A small percentage of children are too abnormal to benefit from the usual run of guidance provision. These are people born with some psychological or physical handicap, or who develop learning difficulties or unacceptable patterns of behaviour at some stage from early childhood onwards; the untreated end-products can range through a dull spectrum of delinquency and crime, neuroticism and personal disturbances of all kinds, sometimes eve a to certifiable insanity, all of which grossly limit the vocational opportunities of their victims. The incidence of maladjustment serious enough to need special treatment among children in England, Wales and Scotland has been found to vary from 3% to nearly 12% in a number of post-war studies carried out in different places (Maclean, 1966). D. Miller (1967) has suggested that about 10% of adolescent at any one time may be showing symptoms of disturbed behaviour. Where the problem is recognized early enough, much can be done to help such cases, but difficult problems of diagnosis, treatment, and sometimes of special education occur. This is the field of the School Psychological Service and the Child Guidance Clinics.

**The Child Guidance Service in Scotland**

In Scotland the educational psychologist is given a more central role than in other countries of Britain, as he is in charge of local Child Guidance Services which combine the functions of the School Psychological Service and the Child Guidance Clinic. Children in need of special psychological treatment (except those receiving private treatment) are referred to the Child Guidance Clinic, which if maintained by the Local Education Authority. When physical conditions are suspected to have some bearing on a child's problems, he is referred to the local Medical Officer, who also refers children to the Guidance Service when he feels a psychological examination to be necessary. Some authorities have established links with the psychiatric services of the Regional Hospitals Boards, and some use the psychiatrist on a consultant sessional basis, cases being referred through the Child Guidance Service itself.

The duties of the educational psychologist in Scotland are therefore very wide. While his training is broadly similar to that of his colleagues elsewhere in the United Kingdom (an honours degree in psychology or its recognized equivalent, training and experience in teaching, and post-graduate training in educational psychology), the Scottish tend to put a high value on teaching experience itself, and on first-hand knowledge of a wide range of classroom problems. Yet, as elsewhere, there are wide differences in the amount of help which can be offered; near cities, teams are often large and well integrated; in remote highland and island regions one psychologist may serve an extensive area. In 1964, only eight out of thirty-five administrative areas had no Child Guidance Service; these were localities where the population was too low in numbers or too scattered to merit a separate Service, and in some, joint arrangements had been made with a neighbouring county.

**Child Guidance Clinics and the School Psychological Service**

It is often very difficult to decide if the causes of a psychological defect are mainly inherited, due: to a physical abnormality, or arise out of the personal history of a child's life. For these reasons some sort of liaison is usually maintained between specialists in medicine, psychology, and education. The School Psychological Service has the difficult job of integrating this work in conjunction with the Child Guidance Clinics. In England, Wales and Northern Ireland, educational psychologists with qualifications in two fields are employed by most Local Education Authorities to deal with unusual learning and behaviour problems in schools, as well as to advise on such matters as selection for secondary education. In 1966 there were over 160 of these School Psychological Services maintained by L.E.A.s throughout England, Wales and Northern Ireland. But the psychologist may also work in a Guidance Clinic, which is by contrast medically orientated. It is usually run by a psychiatrist, and may include a team containing the educational psychologist, a psychiatric social worker, and sometimes play therapists and psychotherapists. The British Psychological Society (1966) classes the functions of the psychologist here as being to aid in the diagnosis of the child's problems; to undertake remedial education where necessary, and to act as a link between the school and the clinic thereafter. Such clinics are well established in 1966 there were over 420 in the three countries mentioned above.

In some regions there is a trend towards linking child guidance more closely with the National Health Service by setting up Child Psychiatric Clinics in association with hospitals. While this makes it easier for the child to obtain a wide range of medical facilities where these are needed (as in cases of psychological trouble arising out of a physical disorder), it does not help much where the root of the trouble is mainly social or educational. Writers such as Isabella Maclean, referred to earlier, feel that such circumstances may tend towards an artificial evaluation of the child as having different problems in different places—whereas the same child is involved in all.

**The Education Welfare Service**

With the growing recognition of the importance of social background, and in particular of the home, in the: development of the individual, services are appearing which concentrate on the improvement of the individual environment wherever this seems to be a major cause of trouble. Of these services, the Education Welfare Service is the oldest, its origins going back to the last quarter of the nineteenth century. We shall look at it first, before going on to glance at some quite recent attempts to broaden the scope of this field of guidance. Every Local Education Authority employs an officer to ensure that children are receiving full-time education according to law; he is generally known as an attendance officer, although the term 'Education Welfare Officer', also used, more accurately reflects current attitudes about the nature of his work. His main job is to visit the homes of children who have not been attending school regularly, and to find out the reasons why. Very often this brings him into contact with major problems of guidance, such as the resistance of parents hostile to education, the total absence of any place in the home where a child can study on his own, and similar inadequacies which in turn make the child reluctant to go to school, or indifferent about work when he gets there. Sometimes also he comes across other specific reasons for a child's absence, such as worry about adjusting to a new and difficult school—especially after transfer from primary to secondary education, or disturbances of adolescence. Again he may have to bring to the attention of the school medical officer a child whom he thinks may need special educational treatment. If he thinks there may be a home problem he can also visit homes even when a pupil's attendance is normal.

This wide range of functions indicates the need for professional training. Often however the officers have no special qualifications in relevant fields such as social work; moreover the amount of guidance which they can give is limited by the opportunities which vary from one local authority to another. Other problems occur because in the eyes of older working-class people, the attendance officer for long represented compulsion and the law. Such officers were first appointed after the Elementary Education Act in England of 1870 as School Attendance Visitors, whose job was simply to drive the children of reluctant parents into school. Their functions were slowly widened through the passing of various Acts during the following decades, but until 1944 officers were still dressed in uniform, with inevitable undertones of coercion. On the other hand, the Education Welfare Service, as the new name implies, has done much to highlight the need for closer links between home and school, and to stimulate such approaches as those which we shall look at next.

**The School Care Committee**

This service is unique to the Inner London Education Authority. For each primary, secondary and special school in the area it provides a staff of voluntary workers to ensure that children are adequately fed, clothed and provided for at home so that they can take full advantage of their schooling. They are selected and advised by professional social workers called School Care Organizers, and work from local offices of the Authority. Regular visits to schools and contact with head teachers is essential for the success of the scheme. The emphasis of the work is clearly upon guidance and welfare rather than law enforcement, and as part of this they keep in touch with pupils up to the age of eighteen, sometimes helping the Youth Employment Officer with specific vocational guidance. An extension of this part of their programme has been to provide advisers to some secondary schools from the ranks of trained social workers, youth leaders and teachers, employed on a paid part-time basis, and forming what is classed as a Young People's Advisory Service. These advisers hold informal weekly discussion groups, are available for private interviews, and also visit the homes of school leavers. The School Care Committees in London are well established, having grown from the turn of the century, with the result that friendly relationships with many families have developed over the years. They also have the advantage of being less associated in the minds of parents with officialdom than other guidance agencies, but a disadvantage is the shortage of trained personnel to fill the ranks of the care workers themselves.

**The Social Worker in School Guidance**

We now turn to look at two fairly recent movements, designed to put the liaison between home and school on a professional basis, and at the closely related concept of the teacher /social worker. These developments represent the forefront of advance in this area, and may well be the pointers to similar provision on a national basis.

In Glasgow experimental attachments of social workers

to schools began in the 1940s, and are now a permanent feature. The workers are administratively controlled from a central office of the School Attendance Department, and in 1966 there were eighteen of them, each based on a secondary or comprehensive school, and responsible to the head master for inter-viewing children and visiting their homes. The advantages of such a system are the speed with which early signs of maladjustment among pupils can be recognized; the expert attention available by a non-teaching member of staff; and the close links that can be drawn between parents and staff. A number of welfare assistants (former school attendance officers) are also employed to assist the school social workers, and to extend the work to primary schools which feed the secondary school with pupils. Routine checks on school attendance are still made by school attendance officers. The work of careers masters and mistresses in this system appears to be limited specifically to careers, and as usual is a teaching post. However, experiments are being tried out with a house master/mistress role which involves some home visiting in liaison with that of the school social worker. For best results, very close links must be kept up between school social workers, house masters and careers teachers. The non-teaching specialist role of the social worker here looks rather like that of the full-time counselor of North America.

Since 1960 an experiment has been going on in Oxfordshire to shift the emphasis from enforcement of school attendance to guidance. A small team of social workers has been appointed, each responsible for a number of non-selective secondary schools, with their contributory primary schools (in contrast to the Glasgow system of one social worker per secondary school). Teachers make the original referrals, and social workers are thus at one remove from the pupils themselves. A. R. Chorlton (1967) opines that this is one reason for the partial failure of the scheme, for some principals have wished to keep matters within the school, or to refer directly to one of the recognized specialists, such as the school psychologist. Some teachers have given the impression that they do not see social workers as professional equals. Is this because of the blurred picture which many people have about social work, aggravated by the piecemeal development of this field, and the continued fragmentation of agencies and training plans? Perhaps a social worker must also be a trained teacher in order to gain acceptance by the teachers themselves.

**The Teacher/Social Worker**

Still fairly revolutionary, the idea that some teachers should be trained in special social techniques, and then given responsibility for visiting the homes of problem children, was stated in the Newsom Report in 1963, and reinforced in a report of the Department of Education and Science the following year; about the same time J.E. Floud proposed a similar idea in 'Teaching in the Affluent Society' (1963). Many other writers have agreed with the principle of teachers visiting the homes of children as part of guidance. A teacher/ social worker has the advantage of being able to talk to teachers as an equal, and to understand the problems of the classroom; as a teacher he gets a chance to know at least some of the pupils in a school; his training in social work helps him to assess family situations, to avoid major blunders in visiting homes, and to maintain contact with other guidance specialists. The question seems to be: Will a part time teaching post leave such a person enough time for adequate home visiting? Will such a hybrid be acceptable to social workers themselves? Will schools, most of which have severe staffing difficulties, be able to carry a teacher with a very light teaching load? Although these problems have not yet been settled, a start has been made at Reading University in training teachers for this dual role. In 1967 an advanced one-year course leading to the Diploma in Educational Guidance with special reference to the Social Environment was set up in the Institute of Education specifically for the training of teacher as school based teacher/social workers. The course is open to qualified teachers with five years' experience and has so far taken about twenty students each year. It has a theory content of sociological studies, and a practical content of visits and attachments.

At Edge Hill College in Lancashire, selected students are offered a three-year course in social work, together with various attachments to social work agencies, and some home visiting. The idea is not to train teachers to do the full work of the social worker, but to give them sufficient skill to be able to assess the nature of a home background problem for later referral, if necessary, to a professional social worker. A one-term in-service course in the same field has also been started for qualified teachers who wish to extend their knowledge along these lines. The idea of, the teacher/social worker seems likely to spread with the growing interest in guidance generally, and it is vital that such teachers should be trained to work reciprocally *with* careers teachers, and not separately or in competition with each other.

**The Changing Concept of Youth Leadership**

The idea of providing a social organisation outside the school where members would be able to develop their abilities and receive indirect guidance in an atmosphere of goodwill and encouragement, dates at least from the foundation of the Young Men's Christian Association in 1844. A vast expansion of this principle during the following century is signposted by many famous names such as the Boys' Brigade (1883), the Boy Scouts (1908), and the Girl Guides (1910). Government support followed, speeded in the 1930s by the threat from Nazi Germany, and in 1939 a Youth Service was formed, to co-ordinate the efforts of voluntary organisations with those of the state and local authorities. In 1944 the McNair Report recognized the need for close liaison between youth leaders and teachers, recommending that service in youth organisations should be linked up with ordinary teaching in schools, and that salaries and superannuation schemes should be comparable and transferable.

The major value of a well organized system of youth clubs is in easing the transition from school to work for the early leaver. Most schools emphasize a high standard of moral conduct, and often contain some teacher to whom the adolescent with problems can turn for advice. This is less often the tradition in work, where a supervisor may be concerned only with output from an employee.; and appear as a remote or even hostile figure to the newcomer. For such people, the youth organisation can offer a return to an atmosphere of benevolent encouragement, and in the youth leader an adult who will listen sympathetically to whatever the member has to say. In this way the leader must from time to time be involved in specific questions about members' jobs, and indeed some of them receive the local Youth Employment Officer as a regular visitor for talks with members.

Today there is a gradual realisation of the value of the club leader as an agent in vocational guidance, and adequate training for such work is a pressing need. In 1961 a Department of Youth Work was formed at Manchester University to give a year's instruction in this field, and recently its functions have been extended to provide specific vocational guidance for young people on a voluntary basis. Another sign of the times was the recent decision of Derbyshire Local Education Authority to second a youth leader for the post-graduate course in guidance at Keele University. Two-year courses in youth leadership are now offered at a number of colleges of education in England. At least one of these courses, at Edge Kill College, emphasizes the specific guidance role of the youth workers.

What of the future? Leaders of thought in this area now see a progressive narrowing of the gap between teachers and youth workers. They believe that all youth workers, as well as having social group work skills, must possess guidance skills. Along with the emergence of the teacher/social worker, the teacher with qualifications in youth leadership and guidance would go part of the way towards implementing the recommendations of the Newsom Report that schools should be linked more closely with the local community.

**Conclusion**

In the general pattern of guidance facilities available today, as well as in new experiments, there seem to be at least three main weaknesses. The need is not covered adequately. The early leaver may not belong to a youth club; may never invite the attentions of the Education Welfare Service or of the School Psychological Service; for most early leavers there is no provision similar to that mentioned in London, Glasgow and Oxfordshire. Many of them have never heard of N.I.I.P. or of the other specialists in careers guidance, and may go out to work after only one talk and one interview with the Youth Employment Officer. Second, there is on the whole little co-operation between the different guidance agencies themselves, such as the School Psychological Service and the Youth Employment Service, both of which are often locally overworked to the extent that they simply do not have time for extensive consultation with each other or with the schools. Third, there is some suggestion of professional distrust between some of the agencies, or between them and teachers, as shown for example in the Oxfordshire experiment described earlier. This lack of useful co-operation has yet to be remedied by general planning to knit the new concepts now emerging, such as those of the teacher/social worker and the guidance specialist/youth leader, into a national pattern. The recommendations of the Seebohm Committee (1968) suggest that: there is some high level concern about the fragmentation of local authority personal social services. In particular they emphasize the need for an enquiry into the organisation of services for young people, which they describe as being vital, and in need of urgent development. In the meantime the diversity of the approaches now being tried out may help us to discover which are best suited to the present and future needs of our society.

The instances taken from the British pattern of guidance services are equally applicable to other countries as well. Though the society, the education and all the more the pupil and teacher have changed over the passage of almost one century, it is still remarkable to make our policies taking lessons from history of the recent past.

# 9

# Guidance Team

> "The test of a good teacher is not how many questions he can ask his pupils that they will answer readily, but how many questions he inspires them to ask him which he finds it hard to answer."
>
> —*Alice Wellington Rollins*

The structure of any such team reflects and reinforces attitudes towards education, as well as towards guidance itself. For example Barr (1958) noted that in American elementary schools the most common approach is to centre guidance on the classroom and the teacher, using specialists only on a referral basis with problems beyond the teacher's scope. Such an approach, he holds, tends to classify guidance and education as synonymous. Much guidance then occurs on an incidental basis; it is closely interwoven with the curriculum and the everyday processes of the schoolroom. Possibly we see something of the same attitude in British secondary schools which lack any clearly defined careers teacher role. The disadvantages of such an approach have been suggested in earlier chapters. Barr goes on to define a second type of structure, commonest in American secondary schools and college programmes, in which guidance is centred on a school counselor, supported by other specialists to whom he can refer problems. He suggests that in such organisations the importance of the individual teacher declines with increasing definition of the specialist role. At the same time guidance tends to focus its attention on unresolved problems and to assume that the development of personality and of educational planning are the business of specialists, with teachers only as helping agents in the process. Such a system, he holds, makes the implicit assumption that only the specialist has the ability to handle problems of maladjustment, and because there are few highly qualified personnel compared with the number of children needing help, is an unrealistic solution. He points out that it is particularly unsuitable as a solution for elementary school guidance, as it tends to take responsibility away from the classroom, teacher who is with the child throughout the school day and is the obvious person to carry out school guidance. Barhas the advantage of drawing on American experience, whose organisation and development of guidance services is a good deal more advanced than in Britain. But the difficulties he outlines might easily emerge in this country, and are worth bearing in mind.

Guidance facilities are not well recognised in our secondary schools; their distribution is piecemeal, and there are many schools without careers teachers, even though here and there one finds complex teams at work. But Daws (1967) thinks that one can make out a slow process of growth towards team guidance. The old-fashioned view was that education and guidance were different and separate; the Youth Employment Officer, located outside the school, was called in briefly and finally to advise leavers about suitable jobs. Daws sees the emergence of the careers teacher role as an expression of the feeling that the school should be involved in the guidance process. This represents an important change of attitude towards the goals of education. The result has been the emergence widely of a two-man guidance team (careers teacher and Youth Employment Officer) together with a broadening of the concept of Youth Employment work. Daws also states his belief that under the influence of the Newsom Report this team is finding increasing help from sympathetic teachers, many of whom accept that the curriculum itself may be fashioned to contribute towards the purposes of guidance. These ideas about curriculum involvement, Daws says, show that teaching and guidance in Britain are becoming integrated rather than separately developed as distinct-processes with distinct aims. This in turn allows the Youth Employment Officer to concentrate on the transition from school to work, and such problems as advising visiting speakers, suggesting visits to workplaces and so on. The concept of guidance as involving personal development follows naturally from recognising it as part of the educational process, and leads towards the appearance of a third specialist, the school counselor. Thus he sees the gradual emergence of a three-man guidance team, out of the present educational system. In this team the school counselor would deal with problem children, including children with home difficulties, with the object of rescuing them before their disturbance becomes serious, and to speed the referral of those needing special medical or psychological attention.

On the other hand, some expert would like to include a specialist social worker or teacher/social worker to deal with home-school relationships. Juniper (1967) believes that the social needs of the community from which the school draws its pupils have a statistically normal distribution, which if shown on a graph would provide a bell-like curve. At one end of such a distribution would lie a few families with no problems; at the other end a few families with difficulties so extreme as to take up most of a caseworker's time. However he thinks that there would be many families in the 'bulge' of the distribution which could greatly benefit from guidance by a school social worker, aimed at preventing minor social problems from deteriorating into major casework ones. Is this a case for a fourth member of a guidance team? Daws forces several difficulties in guidance teamwork: how best to relate member' various approaches to each other; how to establish effective, links with teachers, school heads, parents, and professional and semi-professional workers outside the school, such as educational psychologists and education welfare officers, above all, how to help teachers understand the differences between teaching, guidance and counselling.

**Administrative Relationships**

If guidance services in schools are to develop in an organised manner and not in the piecemeal pattern of the past, they require recognition by Local Education Authorities and acceptance within the general framework of regional educational planning. How might this be done? Hans Hoxter (1964) has offered an interesting solution through the extensive modification of the Youth Employment Service. In his proposals, a new structure of the Service might be based on professional workers in three key roles, those of the School Counselor, the Vocational Guidance Counselor, and the Vocational Guidance Adviser. He would try to obtain intimate knowledge of every member of the group and be accessible to them for individual discussions. He would help parents to understand the educational provisions and vocational opportunities available for their children, and carry out the general work of a careers teacher, as well. Finally he would be responsible for liaison with the Vocational Guidance Counselor.

The Vocational Guidance Counselor would be based outside the school, and serve a number of secondary schools. His duties would include many of those now handled by the Youth Employment officer, such as work with prospective school leavers, and placement of leavers in jobs. Hoxter stresses that the Vocational Guidance Counselor would be a more highly specialised person than his present counterpart in the Youth Employment Service; in particular he should be qualified to use a wide variety of psychological tests of a group and individual kind, as well as being able to employ specialised casework techniques to assist the many young people who need prolonged help in adjusting to adult society. The Vocational Guidance Adviser is seen as a senior official on the staff of all Local Education Authorities. His work would be to plan and co-ordinate the activities of school counselors; to supervise them; to provide material needed in guidance work; to plan in-service training and keep counselors up to date with new developments; to co-ordinate liaison between schools, employers, and professional organisations; and to act as a consultant for counselors, aiding also with the referral of individuals needing psychiatric advice. For the success of the three roles much longer and more intensive training would be required.

An advantage of these proposals is that although a completely new Service is envisaged, many of the existing structures could be retained, and it would be possible to see the change as a growth process. The recent Albemarle Report suggested the deepening of Youth Employment Officers' duties below the last year at school, and proposes that in certain areas a senior tier of experienced officers should be posted, a position which seems to point in the same direction as Hoxter's plans for the work of the School Counselors and the Vocational Guidance Advisers. A major departure from present Youth Employment Service practice is the idea that the School Counselor should be a full time staff member of an individual school, where at present Youth Employment Officers serve several schools in a local area.

In view of the complexity of problems in large secondary schools, the School Counselor would no doubt have to take his place as a member of a guidance team alongside a careers teacher and possibly also a teacher/social worker. This raises important problems of principle and of inter-professional relationships. Should school counselors be specialists brought in from outside? Should they be qualified teachers selected and given further training for this role? What sort of problems arise where specialists trained in different disciplines and distinct approaches to the same problem are brought together as a guidance team?

**Inter-professional Relationships**

When a careers teacher and a Youth Employment Officer are brought together in an embyronic guidance team occasional differences of approach may arise out of the different specialist background and experience of the two individuals. In a larger team these differences could well be more obvious—the school counselor possibly representing the views of psychology, the social worker those of sociology, and the teacher those of education. For effective work close liaison would have to be maintained with other specialists, such as doctors, psychiatrists and administrators, thereby increasing the number of people with different approaches to similar problems.

Unfortunately relationships between members of different professions are not always co-operative or even cordial. McGowan and Schmidt (1962) observed that some professions will respond to a request for consultation but would never think of asking for consultations with those who made the request; others will exchange consultations more freely with persons in different professions; other professions frequently seek advice but are never consulted by the professions which they approach. The suggestion is that a pecking order exists in which well established senior professions may feel threatened by a newly emergent profession which seems to be offering a similar kind of service of a lower quality.

Shoben (1955) believes that for the most part inter-professional struggle takes place at the administrative and official level, rarely at the point where the public is served and the work gets done; but there is always a danger that a disagreement at this level could extend to interfere with casework itself. He makes three points about solving such difficulties. Professional status is conferred by an informed public in recognition of the value of services provided; therefore it is better for a profession to concentrate on giving good service than on developing its power as a pressure group.

Second, a profession should publish statements of what services it offers, its training requirements, and its future goals.

Third, inter-disciplinary discussions about principles and practice should take place at all levels, even though some professions may feel that this is unnecessary. McGowan adds to this that it is the business of competent administration to provide opportunities for friendly discussion, especially among members of guidance teams.

The Seebohm Report (1968) surveying a related field, echoes much the same view; specifically stating that different professions in Britain should begin discussions among themselves and with members of the public to develop a new code of practice, and that central and local governments should provide the administrative framework needed for the code to work. Principles such as these are sometimes difficult to implement. Although communication should prove fairly easy among guidance specialists located in a single school, opportunities would be fewer for contact with school welfare officers, educational psychologists, and Youth Employment Officers, all at present based outside the school. Perhaps this is the area where the barriers to effective team growth would be most formidable; it may well be that in the future the most effective solution will be found in the evolution of many specialist roles within a very large school unit.

**Relationships with Other School Staff**

If we think of a guidance team as something that exists inside an individual school, there is no important administrative reason why teachers and specialists should not establish an informal relationship at the level of individual casework. The careers teacher might form the initial link between team and staff; established and recognised as a teacher by others, he would be well placed to explain the specialist viewpoint. The school counselor and the teacher/social worker would receive many of their problem cases directly from staff members; they would also normally ask the staff for their opinion in building up case studies of individuals.

How would this work out in practice? Here we can do little more than guess; there is not enough evidence from the working of these new roles in Britain to analyse the problems with confidence. Barr noted an important question in the United States, which is raised quite often by teachers in this country: would specialists take over the personal guidance of children so far as to reduce the teacher's role to one of instruction only? Would teachers resent the presence among them of a non-teaching specialist, who might have a private study for interviews and possibly a higher salary? Should such specialists have a part-time teaching appointment? Some teachers point out that this might make them more acceptable to other school staff, and would enable them to get to know pupils more easily. Against this, it might be found that the roles of a teacher and a counselor or teacher/social worker were in conflict; for example it would be very difficult to reprimand a pupil in the classroom and then a few moments later expect him to co-operate in discussing his personal problems in a permissive setting. In the USA this sort of problem has been found difficult to resolve, and it is generally recognised that the two roles of teacher and counselor are incompatible. The trend in American high schools is towards appointing full time counselors with no teaching duties.

**Relationships with Clients**

The word 'client' is an unfortunate one, but it has become the standard term in referring to all of those who receive guidance from counselors or others. Here it is taken to include pupils, students and any one else who might seek advice from the guidance team. In this section we shall look at how far success in such relationships is dependent on rapport between counselor and client, and at how far this can be maintained when guidance is organised along team lines.

Rapport is described by Carkhuff (1967) in terms of an easy permissive relationship between two persons, marked by mutual trust, warmth and receptivity to each other's responses, such as often exists between parents and children, and in other significant human relationships. He believes that counselling and psychotherapy are instances of such interpersonal processes, and that the success of guidance depends on the extent to which this relationship can be established between counselor and client. If this is so, it follows that a guidance team's effectiveness will be greatest where such relationships are most widely developed between members and their clients. But here we have a paradox. Such a relationship is a person-to-person process; it is possible to imagine it existing between clients and individual team members, rather more difficult to visualize its presence between a client and every member of a team; and almost impossible to think of such a relationship developing between a client and anything so abstract as the concept of a team itself. If however the pupil has serious psychological or home problems, the careers teacher might have to pass the case on to the school counselor or teacher/social worker. From this point onwards, guidance might be much more difficult, as it is unlikely that the special relationship could easily be transferred from one person to another. Such a problem might arise from time to time in guidance, as apparently straightforward vocational questions can have very deep roots.

The problem of confidence is closely related to this. The essential relationship for rapport is one of trust, where in seeking solutions to his problems a pupil or parent may disclose the deepest secrets of his life. A permanent record of this must be kept by the team member concerned to ensure continuity of treatment; the main facts must also be available to other guidance staff if effective teamwork is to take place. In this way the confidential information becomes the property of an organisation instead of an individual. Clients, who request specialists to keep certain information secret must be told such facts; this introduces a real risk that the client may prefer to stop coming for guidance rather than accept such a situation.

There are no easy answers to such difficulties. A possibility is that rapport may not be so vital to all successful guidance as Carkhuff suggests. In a summary of some recent work, Eysenck (1965) has pointed out that in curing neuroses the contribution made by the interpersonal relationship between client and therapist varies with the type of disorder under treatment. In certain disorders such as eneuresis the relationship is of no particular significance in determining the course of treatment. In other types of disorder which are complex and long-standing, the relationship is of some significance. A similar variation in the importance of the relationship may well occur in vocational guidance, but more research is needed before we can offer firm evidence.

In this chapter we have been more concerned to define problems than to offer solutions to them. The teamwork is essential to sound guidance, and that the problems involved should be accepted as a first step towards their solution. The only justification for using a guidance team instead of an individual is to offer an improved service to the client. The success of such teams is not to be measured in terms of the complexity of their organisation, the volume of their published work, or in the number of cases treated in a year. If it can be measured at all, and separately from the success of its individual members, it might be through an evaluation of its acceptability, both to its members and those who use its services, after a few years of work.

# 10

# Towards Guidance Movement

> "A great mathematician Bertrand Russel, when asked how he accounted for his many new discoveries in what to the layman seems an already completely explored and fixed science, answered "I challenge the axioms."

Under the benevolent care of teacher children blossom and mature. They are taught a variety of subjects like Mathematics, Science, Social Studies, Mother-tongue, National language, English and also the Fine Arts. School curriculum is framed on the firm foundation of the genesis and development of human abilities. A variety of disciplines contribute to a holistic cognitive development of children. However, as children ascend to higher classes, they realise they are proficient in some and deficient in some other areas. Some students may prefer Mathematics and Science, while some find History and Geography more fascinating. Some pick up languages quickly while others display their virtuosity in Fine Arts. It is a natural phenomenon.

It cannot be ascertained, planting a sapling and water it regularly, the direction in which the branches should spread or the thickness of its trunk or even the fruits it should bear. These are predetermined. But teachers who nurture the growth and development of mental abilities of children year after year ought to be more aware of the direction in which the branches spread. Parents who profess and also repose so much faith in school teachers do not seem as sure about their counsel when told, "Your son/daughter would be an eminent short-story writer or a novelist or an eminent historian or sociologist. They want teachers to say the obvious - that they would blossom into top-ranking Doctors and Engineers. The lure for lucrative jobs deflects many of our bright brains to areas unrelated to their aptitudes. The sane counselling provided by teachers is sidelined by parents when it does. not suit their choice of what their wards should be.

Somewhere a century ago the Guidance-Movement gathered momentum in the American soil. Industrial Revolution profoundly affected the life-style of people. There was a growing demand in the industry for the 'right' person to do the right job. Frank Parsons played the leading role in the USA, who is hailed as the 'Father of Guidance Movement'. That set in motion the support system, namely 'Mental Testing'. Not for nothing did Bennett, Seashore, and Wesman labour hard to prepare the "Differential Aptitude Test (DAT). They sought to study the aptitudes of students at school stage. E.K. Strong designed the 'Vocational Interest Blank' (SVIB) to determine pupils' interests.

Back in India, the Mudaliar Commission set up by the Government of India in 1952 strongly recommended the establishment of Guidance and Counselling Services and Secondary Schools in 1954. It was reiterated by the Kothari Commission in 1966. The Central Bureau of Educational and Vocational guidance was established in New Delhi in 1954. It was later merged with the Department of Psychological Foundations in the NCERT, New Delhi.

For several years the Department in the NCERT offered a One-year Post-graduate Diploma course in Guidance and Counselling. The National Policy of Education (NPE-1986) underscored the importance of Guidance in Education. In spite of all these well-meaning efforts of educationists, our school authorities are yet to realise its importance and establish a Guidance wing, staffed by trained counsellors.

Meanwhile, there is a persistent flow towards certain select professions like computers and medicine. Given an opportunity all students wish to be in these professions, irrespective of the fact whether they have an aptitude for the subjects or not. Parents are the major culprits in this exodus because they systematically brain-wash their sons and daughters and thus contribute to the Brain-drain.

Some instances would illustrate this. Imagine for a moment what would have happened to R.K. Narayan had his teachers and parents coerced him to study Medicine or Engineering! He was not ashamed to be a story-writer though he took a long time to reach the peak. His brother R.K. Laxman chose to be an indifferent student so that he could make caricatures of his teachers by cartoon-drawing. His life was also a successful one.

Why did Salim Ali choose to wander in the countryside to watch birds? Did he not become a great ornithologist? C.V. Raman resigned a well-paid Government job and chose to teach Physics. He planned his life well. Ramanujan, a failed Intermediate boy, did not remain contented with the clerical job in Madras Port Trust. His hobby of Mathematics calculation catapulted him to the zenith of glory. The parents and teachers of these men did not brain-wash them to choose a particular profession.

Instead of thrusting or imposing a profession on their children, parents should work together with the teachers and help their ward realise where his/her aptitude lies. A professional counselling centre would be an ideal platform for this. But, the Guidance Movement is doomed to fail in our country. Just count the number of schools that have employed full-time trained counsellors. Parents are also to blame for this. They would certainly rebel at the intervention of counsellors. After all, don't they presume to know better what is good for their daughters and sons?

Guidance has its positive effects, no doubt, but it may also bear an adverse effect on children.

## Vocational Maturity

Compared to the birds and animals, human beings have a fairly extended period of development from Infancy to Adulthood. Each stage has some developmental tasks to be completed to ensure maturity.

We have a constitutional right and privilege to receive formal, meaningful education upto the age of fourteen years. It roughly corresponds to the end of high-school education. Some might go beyond while others would seek jobs. Those responsible for framing the curriculum for school-education should have the foresight to design a compact package almost similar to the balanced diet one needs for good health.

### *Languages*

India is a multilingual country where there are many regional languages. Therefore, one needs to have a mastery over language. Besides the national and the regional language we need a knowledge of English.

Communicative ability-written and spoken-throws open a variety of jobs for any person, be it journalism, Law, Teaching or as a Salesman, a Doctor or an Engineer. One may have to go to rural areas and address the villagers in their own mother-tongue regarding up infectious disease, Environmental cleanliness and so on.

Those who could communicate well have an edge over those who are poor communicators. If one's job takes him beyond his State he should be proficient in the language that binds people together. We should encourage children to be fluent in more than one language.

*Early Lessons*

Psychologists are of the opinion that a child has the capability of learning more than one language. We should exploit this. The ability to think, reason and judge correctly is a God-given gift. But, it will not develop unless one deliberately cultivates and exercises it. Needless to add how indispensable these abilities are for effective living!

Curriculum-framers have included Science and Mathematics in School education precisely for this purpose. One wonders at the genius of Ramanujan, the mathematical prodigy. One is thrilled by the inventions and discoveries of scientists like Louis Pasteur, J.C. Bose, C.V. Raman, Homi Bhaba, Newton, Einstein, Graham Bell and so on. Each one demonstrated the value of scientific temper. Each one had abundant curiosity.

*Schooling*

As parents we should always urge youngsters to enjoy schooling, like every subject and postpone vocational selection till maturation. Vocational maturity is related to emotional and intellectual maturity. One should not decide hastily and regret late. After all every teacher in school is a specialist in his own discipline. Is it not unfair to look upon -A- as superior and look down upon -B- as inferior, just because A and B teach different subjects? If, as parents, we realise this truth, we would be laying the foundation for a meaningful life for our children.

*Opportunities*

To take up a study of Science opens up many avenues of vocation. One could be a physician, a physicist, an entomologist, an architect, a computer specialist, or a science teacher! Let us not commit the folly of forming a hierarchy and instal one above the others. Imagine how miserable life would have become if every other person were to be a Physician or a Computer specialist. We would have a surplus and that surplus would impoverish society. We do not consider 'rice' superior to 'wheat' or carrot better than beans. Don't we need all these to make life worth living! Let us, therefore, foster the scientific temper among students so that they could choose an area for specialisation after general education.

We have muscles and sense organs. Don't we cheer the athletes in a sportsmeet? Don't we feel proud that our Leander Paes brought a bronze-medal from the Olympic games? Don't we feel elated when Geet Sethi won the billiards championship? Curriculum framers realised the value of sports and games in the development of personality. Instead of becoming slaves of the Cable TV we should go out and play vigorous games. It would be quite refreshing.

It is evident from the findings of Psychological that human Intelligence originates as a general mental ability that is fed by nutrients such as language, computation, cause-and-effect relationship, memorisation and appreciation till about the fourteenth year. Hence, a common curriculum is provided for all children upto SSLC so that the multi-dimensional aspect of intelligence is taken cognizance of.

As one ascends the ladder of schooling, somewhere around the age of 10 or 11, one notices an inclination to study, enjoy and profit from one or two disciplines among his school subjects. It cannot be taken as a crystallized, mature choice based on one's awareness of nature. At best, it can be construed as an act of exploration of one's real interests and aptitudes. These would still be in their incipient stages and perhaps the necessity to study a number of independent disciplines might come in the way of focussing upon a few.

On reaching the school-final stage, a student would, more or less, have made up his mind whether he should opt for humanities or sciences. Here again, it remains broad-based for a couple of years, lending scope for further limitation into fields such as English, Economics, History, Sociology or Commerce under Humanities; Physics, Mathematics, Chemistry and Biology, under Sciences. Yet, he has 'per force' to study a constellation of interrelated disciplines notwithstanding his exclusive interest and aptitude in one or two subjects. At this point he realises he is in a forked-road situation with choices open for professional courses such as Engineering, Medicine, Agriculture and Commerce and for general education courses like Arts and Sciences.

In Indian society there is a tacit notion that Medicine and Engineering constitute the apex of professions and therefore the best of brains have to gravitate toward that direction. It is true that doctors and engineers play a significant role in society while it is not true that others play an insignificant role!

Parents of children with above average intelligence visualise a bright future for their wards either in Medicine or Engineering. Hence, a good deal of brainwashing is systematically perpetrated on young minds that they should strive hard to realise the parental ambitions. Parents worry over the grades and marks much more than the students themselves because any regression in grades is likely to influence adversely their possible entry into these prestigious professions. In this rat-race everyone ignores the natural and spontaneous liking of the youngsters! They are constantly prodded to mirror the aims and aspirations of parents rather than pursuing a course of studies they really desire!

What is the basis of the choice of such professional courses? Very few would admit frankly that it assures them a lucrative career, heightened status and possibly a considerable demand in the matrimonial market too! If the aim is to be imbued with a zeal of Sir M. Viswes-waraiah or Dr. Rangachari in doing Yeomen services to society, zealous youngsters would readily fall in line. But, a really brilliant student may have to crush his desire to study pure sciences like Theoretical Physics or Pure Mathematics for the simple reason he is not assured of a secure future! What if? An Einstein or a Raman or a Tolstoy never had such designs for a rosy future. Did they not plunge themselves into a world of their own and exercise their free-will unfettered by parental designs?

Infact everyone who joins an Engineering College or a Medical College turns out to be a successful engineer or doctor? The mushrooming of these professional colleges and the extortion of phenomenal capitation fees have polluted the academic climate in our country to such an extent that many bright students regret the choice of their studies midway through the course. Quite a number of them feel that they ought to have exercised their options and opted out of such professional courses. The National Laboratories in our country need fertile brains to conduct researchers of far-reaching significance.

# 11

# Guidance and Evaluation: Evolution and Development

"Who teaches me for a day is my father for a lifetime."

—*Chinese Proverb*

Though conventional teaching and guiding methods have undergone a sea change in recent times, it is still significant to illustrate the long march of teaching in historical perspective.

This discussion has basic foundation on recommendation of the Secondary Education Commission.

Basic education was intended to revolutionize all life and activity in the primary school and draw out 'the best in the child—body, mind and spirit. The Secondary Education Commission devoted an entire chapter in its report to dynamic methods of teaching, discussing the objectives of the right techniques, the values of various activity methods and the different ways in which these methods and techniques could be adapted to suit different levels of intelligence. Considerable efforts have been made during the last decade through seminars, workshops, refresher courses and summer institutes to introduce the teacher, especially at the secondary stage, to new techniques of instruction.

The use of audio-visual aids and computers has been on the increase in urban schools, and even television has been brought into the service of classroom teaching in many good school. And yet it will be generally agreed that the impact of these activities on teaching practices in the vast majority of our schools has not been very significant. The picture is particularly dismal in the rural areas, and especially in the primary schools. In the average school today, instruction still conforms to a mechanical routine, continues to be dominated by the old besetting evil of verbalism and therefore remains as dull and uninspiring as before The problem is complex and the answers to it are not easy to give.

(i) *The weakness of the average teacher:* By and large, the competence of the average teacher is poor; this general education is below standard and his professional preparation unsatisfactory.

(ii) *The failure to develop proper educational research on teaching methods:* Little has been done to find out in crucial sectors the methods that are best suited to our conditions and needs. For instance, the best methods teaching beginning reading in a phonetic script like Devanagri have yet to be developed.

(iii) *The rigidity of the existing educational system:* Better methods of teaching are discovered, not so much through educational research, as through the adventures of gifted teachers who have the courage to get off the beaten track. Our educational system is not designed to encourage initiative, creativity and experimentation on a large scale and is, therefore, not able to keep itself abreast of the times.

(iv) *The failure of the administrative machinery to bring about a diffusion of new and dynamic methods of teaching:* Even assuming that a good method of reaching is discovered and is actually introduced in a few progressive schools, the problem still remains of diffusing it among the other schools so that it becomes the common practice in the educational system as such. This is a difficult task, and we have yet to find the right techniques for accomplishing it. We do not propose to examine here the methods of teaching different school subjects as there is a good deal of pedagogical literature available on these topics. It is our considered opinion, however, that the failure to modernize our teaching methods is very largely due to the third and fourth factors stated above—the rigidity of the educational system and the administrative failure to diffuse even known and practised methods among the schools. We shall address ourselves mainly to these two problems in the course of this chapter.

**Elasticity and Dynamism**

In a modern society where the rate of change and of the growth of knowledge is very rapid, the educational system must be elastic and dynamic. It must gave freedom to its basic units—the individual pupil in a school, the individual teacher among his colleagues, and the individual school within the system to move in a direction or at a pace which is different from that of other similar units within the system without being unduly hampered by the structure of the system as a whole. In this process, the freedom of the teachers is the most vital; it is almost synonymous with the freedom of the school, for the pupils can rarely be freer than the men and women who teach them. It will, therefore, be quite an order to equate the elasticity and dynamism of an educational system basically with the freedom of teachers. It has to be remembered that advances in classroom practice never occur on a broad front, with all the teachers and all the schools moving forward in unison. In a school system with a large number of untrained or postly trained teachers, there is need for a solid framework of detailed syllabuses, textbooks, examinations, frequent inspections and well-defined rules. The average teacher who wants security rather than opportunity for creativity may welcome his support. But the work of the best teachers can be crippled if they are not permitted, encouraged and helped to go beyond the departmental prescriptions. The success of an educational reform will depend upon this flexible approach where the good school or the good teacher is able to forge ahead and the necessary supports are provided to the weaker institutions to introduce the reform gradually. The task of the administrator or inspector in such a situation becomes very difficult. He cannot take the easy line of imposing common restrictions on all or be daring enough to give equal freedom to all. We expect him to analyze the strengths and weaknesses of each school and of each school teacher and to help them make the best progress they can. One of the essential conditions for making an educational system elastic and dynamic, therefore, is for the administrator to develop this competence, to discriminate between school and school, between teacher and teacher, and to adopt a flexible mode of treatment for individual or institutions at different levels of development. This alone can help to promote initiative, creativity and experimentation on the part of the teachers. Certain general conditions are necessary to promote this elasticity and dynamism, some of the more important of which are given below:

(i) A teacher or institution will be able introduce innovations more easily if the parents of the pupils know enough about their purpose so as not to have any fear that they will interfere with their children's chances at the final examination. A strong and respected headmaster or teacher can probably best win over the parents by his own efforts; but in most cases, it will be necessary for the Department to help in convincing parents that changes in methods are desirable and officially approved.

(ii) The individual teacher is most likely to try bold changes in teaching practice if there is a feeling of reform in the air and if he sees his small contribution as part of a major social revolution.

(iii) The experimenting teacher must have much more than the passive acquiescence of the school inspectors. He must feel that officers of the Education Department are personally eager to see experimentation and that they are willing, within reasonable limits, to accept a proportion of failures as part of the price.

(iv) The inspectors are the key figures in any reform of classroom practice. They are *Authority*, present and obvious. They should be consulted from the beginning, should know that their criticism and suggestions carry weight, and should be made to feel that the proposed changes are, in some measure, *their* reforms. A school system can be no more elastic or dynamic than the inspectors will let it be. This is why the in-service education of inspecting officers assumes great significance.

(v) The sympathy and support of headmasters and senior teachers must be won quite early in the programme if they are not to dampen all youthful ardour to experiment and explore. They may not want to break new ground themselves. But if they do not feel they are being by-passed and that the new system is not being foisted on them, they can become its patrons, if not its practitioners. There is also much to be gained by winning the approval of teachers' organisations to any movement that increases flexibility in the school system. Individuals will experiment more readily if they feel that experimentation has the general support of the profession.

(vi) Anything that breaks down the isolation of the teacher increases his sense of assurance and makes it easier for him to adventure. The strengthening of the teacher's sense of inner security is a purpose common to all the methods advocated to increase the elasticity or dynamism in a school system. It is the basis of all real reform in teaching practice. There are occupations where a mass advance can be achieved by the invention of new equipment and the issuing of instructions for its use. No worthwhile advance in is possible teaching method unless the individual teacher understands what he is doing and feels secure enough to take the first new steps beyond the bounds of established practice. It is easier for a teacher to do so in a small group than when he is working alone. The success of 'team teaching' in introducing new teaching techniques into some American schools is based on the fact that it is not the individual but the team that is responsible for the planning and execution of new methods. It is our belief that the proposed organisation of a school complex in which the teacher works in a cooperative group is more likely to help flexibility than the present system of isolation.

(vii) Nothing reduces a teacher's sense of security or his willingness to take advantage of freedom so seriously as does his ignorance of the subject-matter he has to teach. If he is only a few lessons ahead of his class he dare take no risks, and finds safety in the old routine of rote memorising. Increasing the teacher's level of general education is, in general, the surest way of ensuring that some of them will adopt livelier and more meaningful methods of teaching. Fortunately, the limiting factors is not so much the absolute amount of knowledge the teacher has but the gap between what he, knows and what his pupils know. Consequently, the easiest place to introduce innovations is in classes I and II. There is also a great advantage in taking the lowest classes of the schools as a starting point for reform, since it is at this level that the greatest 'pupil wastage' occurs through repetition and drop-out.

(viii) When in doubt, teachers will teach in the way they were taught themselves and not in the way they were told to teach. So, if a school system is to become more flexible and teaching methods more lively and varied, it is essential that these qualities be established very early in the *practice*, as well as in the *theory*, of at least some of the teacher-training institutions. A few training institutions at both the primary and the secondary levels should become centres for devising, testing, and adapting methods and materials to be used in the schools.

(ix) Innovations are more likely to occur if there is a ladder of promotion up which the bright young teacher can hope to climb by outstanding service.

(x) Obviously, elasticity or dynamism will be increased if there is a reasonable provision of books, teaching materials, and services that will enable some children to undertake part of their work alone or in groups. There is a limit to what can be expected of the most imaginative teacher if all he has is a bare room, a blackboard, a standard textbook, and sixty pupils. The most pressing needs for a teacher who wants to branch out on new methods are, therefore, a good supply of books and paper, and particularly at the lower levels of school education, some simple tools and materials for making equipment. If some teachers in the more poorly equipped schools are to have a real chance to make use of any freedom they are given, it would seem desirable to have at the disposal of the district education officer a sum of money, not too tightly bound up by regulations, that might be used, with discrimination, in providing the minimum facilities and services to certain schools and teachers who show a special willingness and capacity to adopt new methods and standards of teaching. The amount of such aid should never be so great as to make any experiment expensive and incapable of being applied widely. Too many 'pilot projects' are conceived on such an elaborate scale that they irritate teachers in the average schools and are of little value to the system as a whole.

If measures like those described above can be taken, schools and teachers will have opportunities to venture forth on their own and try out new ideas and experiments. Of course, those that will actually utilize this freedom will be few. But it is these few teachers and schools whose work will put dynamism into the system as a whole and help in raising standards, in breaking new ground and in continually adapting the system to the demands of a changing society.

***The Diffusion of New Methods***

Elasticity in a school system is obviously of limited value unless the good practices developed by a few adventurous teachers or schools are spread more widely through the system as a whole. Unfortunately, this is by no means an automatic process in education, where successful experiments frequently die with the men and women who started them, and where the natural rate of spread of even the more viable innovations is measured in decades rather than in years. It takes a great deal of administrative skill and perseverance to get bold new methods understood and accepted by the body of average and below average teachers, even when they have amply proved their value—and firm proofs of success are hard to produce in education. The difficulties are multiplied ten-fold when teachers are expected to accept, not just a new technique for achieving the old ends, but methods that embody in themselves a new concept of the very purpose of education. That is why it is such a long and burdensome task to convert a school system based primarily on memorisation into one involving understanding, active thinking, creativity and what has come to be called 'problem solving'. Each step is not a step but a leap into the unknown, and the average teacher needs skilled and detailed help, and—what may seem to be a contradiction in terms—sympathetic goading if he is to make it at all. This is precisely the problem that we have to face and solve during the next ten to twenty years. Very little systematic research has been undertaken on the diffusion of classroom practices even in the educationally advanced countries, and practically none in developing countries. The earlier researches of Paul Mort and his colleagues at Columbia University seemed to show that a period of 25 to 40 years was necessary in the United States for anything like full diffusion of a new practice, but the rapid spread of such innovations as the PSSC Physics course (which started in 1957, and is now taken by about 50% of the high school pupils studying physics in the United States) has shown that, under certain conditions, the period can be greatly reduced. This experience and some others of its type seem to indicate that the educational administrator can encourage and hasten the diffusion of new teaching practices in a number of ways, the more important of which are indicated below:

(i) Almost all the factors which render the system elastic enough for the outstanding teacher to break new ground will also make it easier for the mass of average teachers to follow his example. However, mere permassiveness on the part of the authorities will not do the trick. They will need to play a more active part with something that comes nearer to persuasion that to pressure but which still leaves no doubt in the teachers minds that the Education Department and its officers favor certain changes. But it must be done with sensitivity and moderation, or the teachers will come to regard the new methods as the Department's latest fad, and may try to apply them, with or without under-standing, to the detriment of the normal work.

(ii) The main body of teachers will accept new methods mare readily if the immediate goals set before them are limited ones. This means that the methods devised by the brilliant teacher or the subject expert may have to be approached by stages, and that the stage demanded of each group of teachers may vary with their ability.

(iii) The usual devices for in-service training such as refresher courses, workshops, demonstrations, exhibitions of work, and visits of quite long duration to see the new methods at work in pioneering schools should be adopted on a large scale. Used with discrimination and skill, films, tapes or radio can bring whole lessons to quite isolated schools, though not so much for their effect on the pupils as for their usefulness in providing a model of good teaching for the teachers.

(iv) Probably the quickest and most effective way of having new theories accepted is to embed them in the 'tools' of teaching—textbooks, teachers' guides, and teaching aids of all kinds. Some teaching of theory will, of course, still be essential. But it will spring from proposed practices instead of floating airily above them. The extent of the theory and the degree of detail with which the practices are set out will vary with the level of general education of the teachers. In the initial stages of development and with weaker schools, it might be necessary for teacher's guides to go into a fair amount of detail on the series of lessons to be arranged throughout the school years, the methods to be used, the teaching aids to be prepared, the activities to be encouraged, and the tests and techniques of evaluation to be employed.

(v) It inherent instructors, specialised in certain subjects and class-levels of techniques, and working under the general direction of the District Education Officer, are even more vital at the stage of diffusing new

> methods than at the earlier stage of the first experiments.

The technique referred to in the preceding paragraph may be described as the laying down of 'tramlines' on which the average teacher can move forward with confidence in his teaching. This method is different from the traditional practice under which the teacher is given lectures on general principles and is then expected to apply them with no more aid than is given by a mediocre textbook.

It is, of course, the administrator's responsibility to ensure that, while providing 'tramlines' for the mass of the teachers, there is still enough freedom left for the bold few to travel more freely. But with this precaution, there is no doubt that these 'tramlines' of progress are the techniques that will be particularly effective for diffusing new methods. It is obvious that this laying down of tramlines is not a 'once and for all time' business—it requires continuous renewal. When an administrator lays down a set of tramlines with immense effort, he generally finds that his 'progressive' tramlines have become a new 'orthodoxy' and that he will have to start laying them down once again and that there will be the same old resistance for breaking away from the earlier tramlines. But that is an inevitable and perennial problem that every educational reformer must face. The provisions made to enable the outstanding teachers to leave the tramlines will help the rest also to leave them in course of time, while the more adventurous teachers will go still further ahead to fresh fields and pastures new. It will be seen that the essence of our recommendation is that only an elastic and dynamic system of education can provide the needed conditions to encourage initiative, experimentation and creativity among teachers and thereby lay the foundations of educational progress. We firmly believe that the risks of freedom and trust in teachers that are implied in this approach are not greater than those of undue restriction and distrust and they are more worth taking.

We should learn to delegate authority, to trust our teachers, to encourage the capacity for leadership amongst them, to treat every institution as having a personality of its own which it should try to develop in an atmosphere of freedom.

# 12

# Introduction to Counselling

"Where ambition ends happiness begins."

—*Hungarian Proverb*

"Beware of ignorance when in motion; look out for inexperience when in action, and beware of the majority when mentally poisoned with misinformation, for collective ignorance does not become wisdom."

—*William J.H. Boetcker*

Broadly speaking, 'Counselling' includes all of those personal contacts with students by individuals who are consciously attempting to understand and assist them by the specific procedures utilised in personal interviewing. The interview may be extensive or brief. It may involve a great deal of participation on the part of the counsellor, or it may involve situations in which almost all of the initiative rests with the student. Counselling in this sense may or may not be preceded or accompanied by measurement or other attempts to understand the student's background and characteristics. Counselling even in the broad sense, however, must be more specific than mere conversations.

**Definition**

The word "Counselling" is frequently confused with the broader scope of the total personnel programme, with the words "guidance" and "counselling" used interchangeably although their meaning is in no sense similar. By the same token, counselling has come to be thought of as primarily conversation in which advice is given to the student or the student's problems studied and the solution presented to him. This again is at best only one phase or one particular kind of counselling, and not the best kind for most situations.

Beyond these two broad misuses of the term, confusing it with the total programme or thinking of it as "advice-giving,"—there are other limitations placed upon the term by individuals who wish to restrict it to a narrow function which meets the tenets of a particular school of thought. For example, one professional man may say that he is counselling only when the student or the client has full opportunity to say anything he wishes without fear of criticism, does all of the talking, and controls completely what is done in the interview. Any other type of personal contact relationship with the student is not truly counselling. The second professional man, of a different school of thought, may indicate that all counselling must be preceded by diagnosis, that is, a careful study of measured characteristics or case-history information, and that this must be done before any attempt is made to help the student through therapy. This diagnostic information may be said to contribute to the self-understanding of the student but only through interpretation by the counselor of facts about the student. For still others, counselling is restricted to what is called psychotherapy, by which is meant therapy based upon cognizance by the counselor of the emotional factors involved in the students' development, with primary attention being paid to such matters as motivation, frustration, conflict, and compensation.

The truth of the matter is that no one of them is correct. No narrow definition can be given for the function of counselling. Counselling takes place in varying degrees of intensity by varying people. Some types of counselling require information from the counselor and some depend upon emotional release for therapeutic values. Other types of counselling call for information about the student which is gathered through careful diagnostic procedure. Still other counselling situations emphasize the emotional factors more heavily than the conceptual. One may become more proficient in dealing with the individual either by meeting a given kind of problem or by improved ability to understand the total personality.

After such a critical analysis of the mistakes of others in defining counselling, it is hazardous indeed to attempt a definition at this point. Nevertheless, some definition is essential and the following is offered: "Counselling is a personal and dynamic relationship between two people who approach a mutually defined problem with mutual consideration for each other to the end that the younger, or less mature, or more troubled of the two is aided to a self-determined resolution of his problem." This definition attempts to reduce a complex function to rather simple terms. One or two points concerning it should be made, however, as an outgrowth of developments in the field since this definition was proposed. The "personal and dynamic relationship" is to be thought of as a purposeful relationship, not a casual one. Not all verbal exchanges between teacher and student on subjects of mutual interest, for example, are to be thought of as counselling.

The one person must desire assistance on matters which affect him personally and the other must have the purpose of giving such assistance before an effective counselling relationship exists. To make the counselling experience meaningful, the counselor must possess qualifications of maturity, experience, and social sensitivity in addition to the *desire* to help. The situation may be informal, but the desire to secure help and to give help must be present in the two parties. The definition makes explicit also that the relationship is a two-way affair, one in which there is mutual contribution by both parties to a possible solution.

It is not a one-way flow of advice and opinions from counselor to counselee. Off-the-cuff solutions and snap judgments may be momentarily impressive but they do not constitute counselling. The client is aided to a solution, and the methods used in giving such aid may vary widely from client to client. In one case the aid may be in the form of a careful appraisal of aptitudes and characteristics, and an interpretation of these findings offered to the client in as skillful a manner as possible.

In another case the skill may rest entirely in the counselor's ability to reflect client attitudes and feelings and in this way to assist him in self-clarification of thought and attitude. The provision of aid does not assume a neat package of diagnosis and solution presented by the counselor. In some cases the aid may be to provide a situation for self-expression where the counselor "stands by" while the client works on himself.

*Counselling is a dynamic and purposeful relationship between two people in which procedures vary with the nature of the student's need but in which there is always mutual participation by counselor and student with the focus upon self-clarification and self-determination by the student.* It is apparent in this definition that the objective of counselling is a self-determined solution or a self-decision upon the part of the student. The function of the counselor is to assist the student to insight and decision so that he, the student, is better equipped to make similar decisions in the future. The counselor's function is to provide for an analysis of the situation, understanding, suggestions of alternative solutions, and an outlet for self-expression and release, each in varying degree from client to client. All of this is to the end that the student himself be better equipped, through release and clarification, for some effective immediate adjustment and more mature future behavior.

**Clinical Counselling**

The term "clinical counselling" is used to designate

counselling which attempts to understand the total individual personality and to deal with this personality through appropriately professional procedures. The word "clinical" is derived from the medical clinic where a number of types of information or a number of specialists, or both, make their particular contribution to an understanding of an individual. The word "clinical" in its medical meaning is therefore not too far afield from its use in psychology. In particular, it specifies carefulness in diagnosis and carefulness in treatment. In such counselling process, the counselor secures information of various sorts in as accurate a manner as possible and analyzes the relationship between these various kinds of information as they may contribute to an understanding of a functioning personality. He may call upon other specialists for their particular understanding of the person, or he may confer with them as to the help to be given. Most of all, however, the term suggests that the kind of counselling done is of a professional nature demanding training and skill and a high degree of individuality in the procedures used with a given client.

Such a concept does not come full-blown into being. It has a long history in the struggle of psychology toward a better understanding of the behavior of man, and in the struggle of individuals in schools, colleges, industry, social agencies, and psychological and psychiatric clinics toward a better understanding of the most effective psychological procedures. As mentioned earlier, the concept most frequently associated with the term counselling is that of "guidance" and, more specifically, this has often meant "vocational guidance."

Psychologists in the early of last century were more concerned with testing reaction time and sensory discrimination than they were with understanding personality characteristics. As a consequence, vocational guidance turned quite definitely toward the field of vocational information and toward attempts to understand the environment and the demands of the vocation. This is a significant phase of vocational guidance and has led in more recent years to job analysis, job descriptions, and the determination of job families. When these are stated in psychological terms, the requirements of a vocational field become immediately comparable with the psychological characteristics discovered in the counselling situation. Vocational guidance, however, calls for analysis of the person and his characteristics as well as for the appraisal of the vocational environment and its demands. It would have arrived at a mature state with an appropriate combination of these two types of information much more rapidly.

The work done in World War I with group intelligence tests, trade tests, and rating scales contributed to a movement which heavily emphasised the use of psychological measurements. Improvements in personnel procedures were also taking place during this period in both industry and schools. With industry having received its start before the war in the work of Magnus Alexander and his studies of labor turnover, the period following World War I was one of rapid advance in more scientific personnel work. This was signalised in the development of the Personnel Research Federation and the Psychological Corporation, with their contributions of research and consulting services to industry. Still later in the field of industrial personnel have come such marked contributions as the better understanding of the importance of the worker's acceptance as an individual in industry, that is, a sense of status and of being personally identified. An emphasis in this direction was a result of the studies at the Hawthorne plant of the Western Electric Company.

Considerable strides have been taken in industry in matters of selection, in the application of job studies to employee hiring, in promotion and salary schedules, in the use of rating scales, and in other procedures which have their direct implications for educational counselling. Educational workers are prone to think that the development of educational procedures has been the product of experience in schools and colleges alone. The contributions of industrial personnel work to personnel procedures in general has not been sufficiently emphasized. The professional field of education has also contributed to our present understanding of counselling.

Education, from the first emphasis upon "individual differences" to the present attempts to offer a varied school curriculum and to provide school counselling services, has contributed a great deal to both understanding and procedures. Remedial reading and the various clinical procedures designed to assist students with educational handicaps is a direct outgrowth of the school programme. To a considerable degree the changes in the purposes of the school have forced attention upon procedures contributing to an understanding of the individual. The study of the school child and the adolescent has been the focus of either workers in the schools or of psychologists and social workers who study children in the schools.

It has operated through such procedures as the establishment of the Measurement and Guidance Committee in the 1920's, the Hopkins Survey of Student Personnel Procedures in 1926, the development of cumulative record forms, rating scales, scholastic aptitude and achievement tests in the late 1920's and the early 1930's, and a Conference on College Personnel Work in 1937 which resulted in the formation of a standing Committee on Student Personnel Work. The later work of this committee and of the earlier Committee on Measurement and Guidance has been very significant. One cannot read far into the history of college personnel work without repeatedly coming into contact with the American Council on Education. One may discover it either as a coordinating agency for some study or as the direct agency performing the study or providing the service in the field of college personnel work.

Psychology has, of course, made the largest single contribution to personnel work. The emphasis, upon objective measurement by Cattell, the early work of Binet on intelligence, and the later work of Terman and Otis on group intelligence tests is followed by a galaxy of test specialists who became famous during the 1920's and the 1930's. Such men as Thorndike, Terman, Thurstone, and Wechsler, as Truman Kelley, Ben Wood, Crawford, and Linquist, as Strong, Bingham, and Paterson, as Woodworth, Symonds, Darley, and Guilford, as Samuel Beck and Bruno Klopfer have brought testing in its many-phases to its present high level of contribution to the understanding of a person. There are many weaknesses still in objective psychological measurement, as will be seen in later discussion, but it has contributed to clinical counselling more than any other single procedure.

A second contribution of psychology has been made through *a* better understanding of the dynamics of the individual. This goes back to the work of G. Stanley Hall and his studies of adolescents and to the work of Sigmund Freud and all that psychoanalysis has meant in the ensuing decades. Of more recent years, the work of Henry A. Murray of Harvard and others in what has been called dynamic psychology, and of Gordon Allport in his individual psychology, demands greater attention in the next section. Nor should the impact of Gestalt psychology with its creed of "the whole is greater than the sum of its parts" be forgotten. The third great offshoot of psychological effort has been in the field of direct psychotherapeutic procedures themselves, that is, in the work of child guidance clinics and the clinical psychologists who have laboriously wrought out present-day procedures.

Many of the procedures used by psychotherapists have been developed through trial-and-error procedure at the cost of time and of human happiness, but others have been the results of careful thought and logical analysis of possibilities before procedures were used or developed.

**The Personality Gestalt**

The dependence of effective counselling upon the concept of the total interrelatedness of the personality has been earlier suggested. This concept and how we arrived at it is so important that it should be given more careful attention. It is not enough to say that we must deal with a dynamic totality; we must also know just what has been the trend toward an understanding of this concept. "Personality is today conceived of in terms of structures rather than traits. There is an attempt to study the individual as a whole, rather than to isolate very small elements for study. Behavior is considered as an interaction of person and situation, rather than as a property of the person alone." What has been the development of this modern concept?

It has been mentioned that psychoanalysis has made a very large contribution to clinical counselling. This is true because psychoanalysis first emphasised certain factors now widely accepted by all who deal with individuals in counselling terms. The proposal that adult peculiarities or characteristics have their origins in childhood experiences is now a part of orthodox child psychology, yet it was first emphasised by Sigmund Freud in his early work in psychoanalysis. While working with Charcot, the great French psychologist, Freud came to the conclusion that there must be other causes of insanity than those physiological in nature upon which the abnormal psychology of that period was based. As a result of a great ideal of experience in relating this theory to individual cases, he developed the concept of a psycnogenetic origin of many types of adult behavior. This is now an accepted tenet of all psychotherapy, and yet it had its birth only some sixty years ago. Similarly, we now accept the theory that many drives and desires are repressed only to appear later in forms of behavior different from that in which the original drive would normally be expressed. This is so commonly accepted an hypothesis that many mechanisms of behavior, labeled rationalisation, compensation, or projection, are commonly referred to by laymen. Perhaps most of all Freud contributed to the idea that the individual is a total functioning organism and that to understand the totality we must understand each given part of the whole and each past experience.

Henry Murray in his excellent volume *Explorations in Personality* stands as an exponent of what might be called the school of dynamic psychology. In this exposition he is concerned with the point of view in psychology which he calls the point of view of the "centralists" as opposed to that of the "peripheralists." Murray attempts to prove that those who have studied personality in terms of its peripheral or exterior manifestations have been guilty of studying it piecemeal. Such psychologists are to be contrasted with those who study the personality as a dynamic whole and who are more concerned with internal drive than they are with external manifestations. This centralist or dynamic point of view in psychology contends that no segment can be seen or understood in isolation from the whole. This is to say that no partial knowledge of a man, such as his scores on an intelligence test or the results of a test of basal metabolism, can be understood apart from the balance of the psychophysical organism which we call a personality.

Murray contends that while it is true that we know much better how to measure accurately the peripheral factors than the central factors, the most significant factors *are* the central ones, that is, those of drive and of integration. Without identifying oneself with any particular school, it is possible to hold the point of view that the personality is a dynamic whole and that the part must be seen in relation to the whole. When this view prevails, any item of case history or any test datum gains its significance from the context within which it exists. This would also imply that no element of the human personality is static. When any element of the situation changes, some phase of the total personality, and therefore the pattern itself, changes. This makes clinical counselling a far more complex and at the same time a far more meaningful operation. The weight of empirical evidence is in the direction of a dynamic, that is, changeable, totality within which the various known characteristics of behavior exist. One cannot take any number of specific facts about the person and add them up in a quantitative fashion to secure a meaningful understanding of the whole. By the same token, the interpretation of specific information about the individual must always be referred back to the clinician's concept of the total personality, even though only dimly understood. For this reason, clinical counselling is dependent upon a combination of judgment and experience, which may be called trained insight. This insight must accompany even the best technical skills in the interpretation of measurement data or the interpretation of a particular behavior cue observed in the interview.

The term "intuition," appropriately used, describes an intangible that enters into any counselling which attempts to apprehend the personality whole. This same quality may be called clinical judgment. It involves the use of cues from data and from personal observation of the client which are not logically followed through from point to point. Intuition in this sense is said by Oldfield to be consolidated resultants of previous experience. A conclusion is based upon cues taken from the information available, but previous experience allows a skilled counselor to short circuit the logical process of consciously reasoning from cue to cue. Another term is that of "insight," sometimes used in connection with the self-understanding of the student, sometimes referring to counselor understanding.

**Counselling Performance**

Whether understood as a broad or narrow process, casual observation of counselling on a college campus leads to the conclusion that almost everyone participates in counselling. Almost everyone, from the maintenance and clerical workers to the president of the institution, has repeated personal contacts with students, contacts which lead frequently to a counselling relationship. Many educational workers are in the field because of their desire to be of assistance to others, their enthusiasm for youth, and their pleasure in seeing young people grasp ideas and use them. For this reason it is almost impossible to separate the function of counselling from the varied functions of all educational workers.

There is a great difference, however, in the degree to which this function is carried out and the skill and completeness with which the task is performed. Clinical counselling, as described in preceding sections, is a task calling for a great deal of skill backed by training and certain personal qualifications. Not every teacher, however active, and not every administrative officer, however interested, will necessarily make a good counselor. They may be good teachers or administrators because they possess the necessary skills, but those skills do not insure good counselling. Conversely, not even good training will make a good counselor if he is lacking in intellectual flexibility, emotional maturity, and an unselfish interest in others.

*Levels of Counselling*

Counselling is performed at different levels of intensity and complexity. If one considers all types of casual relationships between college workers and college students as the first level of counselling opportunity, then the second level might be considered those contacts which take place at the time of registration. A somewhat smaller number than in the first instance, perhaps only a portion of the faculty, participate in advising students with regard to choice of courses and the planning of their course of study. The faculty who so serve act as "advisers." This term is frequently used accurately, since much of what is done at this time is advising the student regarding choice of courses in terms of the requirements of a particular college or curriculum. It is advice in the strictest sense of the word. There is no time, and often no desire, to go very deeply into the student's needs and to do a job of counselling which is more than superficial. Some of these advising experiences develop later into a much deeper relationship between the adviser and the student. On the whole this is more specialised "counselling" than casual contacts, but is still not very intensive.

If one moves arbitrarily from the second to a fourth level of counselling, the latter level would be defined as the type of counselling done by a fully trained individual who spends all or most of his time at this task. It is at this level that there is responsibility, time, and training for doing a more complete job of clinical counselling. The resources may be at hand, in terms of both training and equipment, for going as fully as the situation demands into the needs of the given individual and for administering therapy skillfully. Workers at this point use the various resources of the university intelligently, as either a means of better understanding or of better development of the individual student. The third level of counselling has been described as that done by carefully selected faculty workers.

These, because of both interest and personal qualifications, and perhaps a higher degree of training, are relieved from some portion of their ordinary teaching or administrative load to work more intensively at the job of counselling students. They function under the leadership and with the assistance of the fourth level individual or individuals. They are, in a sense, an extension of his skill and training, and it is his task to see that their counselling effectiveness is increased by whatever means he can use to improve their skills in working with the students. These faculty counselors may undertake to deal with almost any type of problem or need the student may have, although either their time or their training may limit them as to how deeply they can go into complex counselling needs. They are not, however, limited to problems of academic adjustment as is the registration adviser. They should know thoroughly the campus resources that are available in the health service, placement service, admissions office, deans' offices, student activities office, and counselling center and should utilize these resources wisely with each student.

*Organisation of Counselling*

Such an organisation of counselling facilities is based upon the premise that all of the staff of an institution counsel students but not all counsel in the same manner. Trained and specialised counselors work with students on complex and long-term needs, while administrative staff and faculty counsel more often on specific needs and at a lower level of intensity. Lloyd's description of the personnel programme at Brigham Young University and that by Bailey and others of the counselling functions at the University of Illinois make this point clear.

Counselling is not simply one of many personnel functions; it is one performed by both faculty counselors and specialists in the field at different levels of complexity and completeness.

The issue of generalists versus specialists in counselling is listed by Brumbaugh as one of five major issues in the administration of student personnel work. This is not a fundamental issue except as it is made one by those who have not given sufficient thought to a realistic consideration of the situation. The only problem involved is the utilisation of many types of educational workers who perform counselling in either broad or specific areas and at either high or low levels of both diagnosis and therapy. It is not a question of *either* faculty *or* specialists, but of both groups working at their respective levels of student understanding and of counselling procedures. Faculty may be used part-time as semitrained counselors, that is, faculty who are carefully selected and given the benefit of in-service training, often with release of time from some portion of their teaching or committee responsibilities. This is specifically suggested in the University of Illinois programme, in the conclusions of the Counselling Section of the National Conference on Higher Education, and in a number of progressive college programmes not reported in the literature. Kamm and Wrenn in a 1946 survey of the 155 four-year coeducational colleges and universities in the North Central Association, with 70 per cent of the total reporting, found that all but one of the institutions have specific provisions for the counselling of students, although only 67 per cent listed the use of full-time or professional counselors. In many instances in this study it was reported that the number of professional counselors was sufficient to supply less than half of the actual need.

The 67 per cent was an increase, however, over the proportion of institutions making specific provisions for counselling as reported by Haggerty and Brumbaugh in 1938. With this concept of counselling it is seen that the *function* of counselling has a direct line relationship to the dean of students, even though much of this function may be performed by those who bear no line responsibility to him. It is the responsibility of the dean of students to see that the clinical and other specialised counselors are used as effectively as possible on the campus. What is done by everyone else on the campus, including the faculty, is a matter of coordination by the dean of students rather than one of line responsibility. Much is done by everyone, but on many campuses not enough will be done except under the most ideal circumstances of encouragement and assistance from the trained professional workers on the campus. It is not the function of the professional counselor to attempt to do all of the counselling, but to see that the greatest possible assistance is given to the faculty and administrators who, by virtue of their relationship with students, act as counselors. This problem of counselling organisation is analysed at some length by Spindt, who would place all faculty advisers under a dean of students but would have this dean of students in turn under the dean of the college. This would seem to be a confusion of the instructional and student personnel functions and therefore undesirable.

Earlier it has been suggested that the dean of students has a *staff* relationship with the faculty advisers who are actually working under the dean of the college in their major functions of instruction. Careful consideration of this distinction in line-and-staff relationships in the total performance of counselling on a university or college campus is too frequently lacking. The problem is more acute with the larger institutions, while the smaller college is less concerned with problems of organisation and more with the most effective use of techniques.

Frequently the trained psychological counselor, or counselors, will serve through a centralised student counselling service. This may have various titles but the primary function is that of serving as a campus-wide agency for students and as a resource agency for faculty people who are themselves dealing with students. The student counselling center is responsible to the dean of students. The counselors of this bureau may stimulate faculty counselling programmes in various colleges, since theirs is a much wider responsibility than merely that of the counselling performed in their own offices. It is to them that the rest of the campus must look for leadership and for performance, in an effective sense, of the functions of diagnosis and therapy. The counselling center is sometimes the agency which administers the institutional test programme for all new classes. It supplies the information derived from these tests in some interpreted form to the administration and to the faculty who deal with these students in classroom and administrative contacts. It should be repeated that the work of the trained counselor involves the leadership of others as well as the performance of counselling at its highest level of skill.

*Counselling Assistants*

A development of the past two decades is the systematic use of older students as informal counselors of new students or of students in dormitories. Some institutions have used this counselling resource with conspicuous success. Much depends upon the care used in the selection and training of student assistants and upon the extent to which the limitations of their responsibility is defined. Obviously students appointed to counsel other students are neither as mature as faculty nor as cautious in influencing student attitudes and decisions.

The writer visited one campus as a consultant where a dangerous situation was discovered. The dean on this campus had taken wholeheartedly the suggestions made in a summer school course and late in the summer had appointed a considerable number of seniors as counselors of new students. Without the careful selection which should have taken place the preceding spring, without having received preparation for their task during the spring and summer, and without appropriate cautions as to limitations on their functions, these enthusiastic student counselors had dealt directly with programme planning, emotional problems, and home relationships! It was apparent to the writer when he met with the group that only sheer luck had saved them from serious errors. He counseled immediate caution and indicated that their appropriate role was that of acting as a listening station and a switchboard to the appropriate staff personnel.

A great deal of advice and "dope" is passed on to the new student by the old student anyway, and it is constructive to educate and channel this contribution. Students may become aware of other students' difficulties much sooner than staff. If they are charged with responsibility to do so and have been informed as to procedures, they can supply the student with accurate information or refer him to the proper source for help in a very effective manner. Frequently students will confide bewilderment or ignorance to another student that they would be hesitant to tell a member of the faculty or counselling staff. Some colleges have prepared excellent handbooks of instruction and information for use by their student counselling assistants.

**Summing Up**

Counselling is one function of a student personnel programme which is characterised by a face-to-face relationship of counselor and student in which the counselor tries to understand and assist the student in such a manner that the focus is upon student self-understanding and self-decision. "Advising" is counselling in only a limited sense for in this the adviser assumes responsibility for seeing that the "best" decisions are made. Clinical counselling is careful, professional counselling in which information from various sources is skillfully interpreted and in which the interview relationships between student and counselor are handled with equal skill. More attention has been devoted to interpretation than to the interview, but even so, the emphasis may be upon the emotional factors involved in self-understanding. It is not strictly an intellectual process on the part of the counselor, as might be true in its medical counterpart, for in psychological matters the understanding of himself by the client is essential to behaviour or attitude change. Careful counselling has been contributed to by developments in vocational guidance, psychological measurement, industry, and education.

Equally significant have been the contrasting developments of psychological measurements of all kinds and the concept of a unified dynamic personality whole which cannot be divided into segments for measurement! This paradox is not yet resolved except as separate measurement and other data are unified through clinical judgment. Intuition or judgment must fill in the gaps between diagnostic data. There is no statistical device for coalescing parts into a dynamic whole even though statistics are vital to the valid use of the parts.

## *REFERENCES*

Bailey H.W., Gilbert W.M., and Berg I.A., "Counselling and the Use of Tests in the Student Personnel Bureau at the University of Illinois," *Educational and Psychological Measurement*, 6:37-60 (Spring, 1946).

Brewer John M., (1942) *History of Vocational Guidance*, Harper and Bros., New York.

D. Feder, Daniel "Selection and Training of Faculty Counselors," william M. gilbert, "Training Faculty Counselors at the University of Illinois," Donald J. Shank, "Some Questions About Faculty Counselling," John L. Bergstresser, "Issues in Faculty Counselling," *in Trends in Student Personnel Work*, E.G. Williamson (ed.), University of Minnesota Press, Minneapolis, 1949, pp. 288-311.

E.G. Williamson, *Counselling Adolescents*, McGraw-Hill Book Co., Inc., New York, 1950

Hahn Milton E. and Malcolm S. Maclean, *General Clinical Counselling*, McGraw-Hill Book Co., Inc., New York, 1950.

Herbert Hawkes, "Student Counselling," in *Current Problems in Higher Education*, Ralph W. Mcdonald (ed.), Department of Higher Education, National Education Association, Washington, 1947, pp. 111-34.

Hawkes, Mrs. Herbert, "Student Counselling," *Current Problems in Higher Education*, Department of Higher Education, National Education Association, Washington, 1947, pp. 111-22.

Haggerty W.J.and Brumbaugh A.J., "The Student in College and University," a reprint from the *North Central Association Quarterly*, 13: 559-630, 14:201-26 (April and October, 1939).

Kamm Robert B. and Wrenn C. Gilbert, "Current Developments in Student Personnel Programmes and the Needs of the Veteran," *School and Society*, 65:89-92 (February 1, 1947).

Monroe W.S. (ed.), *Encyclopedia of Educational Research,* The Macmillan Co., New York, 1950, pp. 1312-20.

Oldfield R.C., *The Psychology of the Interview,* Methuen and Co., Ltd., London, 1941, pp. 38-41.

Roethlisberger F.J. and Dickson W.J. (1939), *Management and the Worker,* Harvard University Press, Cambridge.

Spindt H.A., "Various Plans for the Administrative Organisation of Faculty Advisers," *Journal of American Association of Collegiate Registrars,* 17:89-92 (October, 1941).

Wrenn C. Gilbert, "Certain Industrial Research Having Implications for Student Personnel Work," *Report* of the Eighteenth Annual Meeting of the American College Personnel Association, 1941, pp. 80-88.

# 13

# Fundamentals of Counselling

"Consider how hard it is to change yourself and you'll understand what little chance you have trying to change others."

—*Arnold Glasow*

"Instead of saying that man is the creature of circumstances, it would be nearer the mark to say that man is the architect of circumstance. It is character of circumstance. It is character which build an existence our of circumstance. From the same materials one man builds places, another hovels; one warehouses, another villas; bricks and mortar are mortar and bricks until the architect can make them something else."

—*Thomas Carlyle*

Counselling is a process of initiating and reinforcing a helping relationship to enable planned growth of the client at his own. Sometimes help and counselling are used interchangeably, though they are entirely different concepts. Helping process may aid at an outcome of reaching an understanding of the client by the counsellor. Helper may not necessarily has to have concern for clients development. His help may remain as a routine activity. Help could also be the extension of dealing with one's own anxiety therefore process of help may not lead towards counselling as such.

**Management Counselling**

Management Counselling for entrepreneurial development

may be understood as a 'counselling process for the institutions to promote the entrepreneurs in the given locality.' It encompasses broad counselling activities, by the institutions focussed on the counselling approach for the development of entrepreneurs.

Objectives of management counselling depends on the nature and level of client. Since the client is entrepreneur the objective may be examined as follows:

(i) To understand the entrepreneurs' nature of background, personality, knowledge and skills etc.

(ii) To understand the entrepreneurial environment in which he operates.

(iii) To diagnose the problems of the entrepreneurs in the pre-investment and post investment stage.

(iv) To diagnose the clients' potentialities to initiate and handle the enterprise successfully.

(v) To enable the client explore this commitment towards his own goal and action plan for enterprise building.

**Counselling and Consulting**

Counselling process imparts an opportunity for the consultant to enable the counsellee to plan put his own plan of action in the given socio-physical, space. The consulting may be accepted as a broad action process where counselling may form of small but significant part. Consultation is a process of seeking or giving professional help. In its broader connotation, the goal of consultation is learning, growth, change and well along the path of problem solving, a problem solution. It may be divided into phases.

Conventionally need for counselling arises after problem has been diagnosed and some action has already been taken by the client as per the pre-counselling help extended to client by the consultant. However there is hardly any definite 'layer' to delineate the stage where from counselling should begin or cease to function. It entirely depends whether consultant assumes the counsellor's role in the given time frame to help the client. Counselling is needed even-in pre-investment stage of entrepreneur to furnish relevant information while completing the prerequisites of the project. The potential consultant largely functions as a legitimised listener and question asker, sometimes as an enquiry expert.

**Nature of Counselling**

Counseling can be both of directive and non-directive in nature. The non-directive counselling is largely client oriented where counsellor listens and records what he listens and uses the information he gets to help dispel anxieties. He does not discipline client in order to control him. Instead the approach is non-paternalistic and counsellee centered. As a matter of fact counselling for entrepreneurs has largely to be of non-directive nature.

Essentially, the non-directive approach in counselling is designed to provide opportunity for the counsellee to work through his problems to his own satisfaction without being given advice or guidance. Here the counsellor establishes rapport and listens people more than talks. Some counsellors consultants find the non directive approach difficult because it does not allow them to advice, argument, lecture or cross-examine.

*Non-directive counselling* demands that the counsellor be secured and well adjusted himself and that he be a good and interested listener who can use a language level appropriate to the occasion without losing the dignity of the counselling relationship. If the counsellor can get the counsellee to state his problem, to give its history, and to develop the problem—without having to ask leading questions—he has developed quite an art. In case of non directive counselling the counsellor takes an active part in bringing about an understanding or solution to a problem. He does not give the client to the solution but directs him towards a solution.

Sometimes client is made aware of that his action would lead toward solution. Now the question arises as to what kind of counselling is required for the entrepreneurs. Institutions prefer a directive counselling method in case the counselling is needed. Controlling through disciplinary action, results into a voluminous follow-up responsibility of the institutions in the post investment stage.

(i) The entrepreneur develops an understanding about himself.

(ii) The entrepreneur develops an understanding about the environment.

(iii) The entrepreneur sets directions for the growth in the context of the above.

(iv) The entrepreneur develops a plan of action, and implements it at his own.

(v) The entrepreneur learns to review it periodically alongwith his counsellor.

(vi) The entrepreneur sees his own strength and weakness and attributes failure or success to himself and reduces dependency on the institutions.

**Counselling Skills Application**

For any counselling to be effective, it is necessary to build a climate of openness between the counsellor and the counsellee. Counselling may take place every day at an informal level between the officers and the entrepreneurs. However, in organisations where appraisal interviews are formally organised, such interviews may give an opportunity for both of them to sit together and discuss various matters relating to performance. During such a discussion, the officers may use his counselling skills to help the entrepreneur develop. Some skills are required by the officers to help the entrepreneur positively in both informal and formal counselling situations. This assumes importance even in medium size enterprises in particular.

Preparation on the part of the counsellor and the counsellee involves investment in terms of time and thinking. If either of them is not prepared to invest in preparating for helping each other and learning from feedback, the counselling is likely to be futile. The counsellor should prepare himself well for making counseling effective. However, the agencies (especially the voluntary agencies which are engaged in entrepreneurship programme need to have a continuous counselling mechanism. District level institutions also encounter entrepreneurs and it may require an institutional mechanics to cater to their counselling requirement of the entrepreneur. Informal counselling may be taking place in organisation quite often between officers and entrepreneur during their interactions.

In this process, quite often the attempt to officer to counsel the entrepreneur is perceived as inadequate or overdone. Such gaps occur because what is thought by the officers as helpful to the entrepreneur may be seen by the client as not meant for him or meant for officers own interest. This is an indicator of a one way process in counselling. The counsellor will therefore do well in preparing for the situation and thinking about that is helpful from the point of view of the counsellee.

**Follow-up Concept**

Follow-up is a process to enable the client understand and realise where does he (client) stand vis-a-vis his enterprise building process. The relations between the institutions and the entrepreneur necessarily dos not remain the same. It undergoes change. Nature and dynamics of change depends on the purpose that we envisage for the follow-up.

The complexities of follow-up procedure is much debatable issue but the objectives are generally accepted by all those engaged in EDP. Follow-up in EDP therefore, is, more of counselling and facilitating their movement towards enterprise development. Dilemmas that training institutions have been facing whether follow-up responsibility is to be entrusted to funding organisation or training institutions? To what extent other colloborators can lend their support in the mechanics of follow-up? Whatever may be the case, colloborator maintains its own tool, a great deal of help can be rendered to entrepreneurs after the course.

'Log-book', a commonly accepted tool by the institutions, can easily be recorded regularly by the field officer or instructor. Each candidate may have its own 'pages' in log-book. The frequent visit and available information about the candidate may be updated at appropriate interval. It becomes a ready reference and very handy tool of follow-up for training institution. even other colloborators can maintain a similar register for each course that they colloborate. 'History Card' Method is another instrument for the organisations who can afford to have better information system. History Card denotes a typical cardex system where we can have prompt and closer look at entrepreneurial progress.

Still there are very few institutions in the country maintaining sound follow up system. Even those who have proven higher success ratio largely depend on the supportive action of colloborating institutions. The 'log book' or cardex system' over a period of time have become routine activity and ritual for some of the organisations. Organisations show excitement at the early stage subsequently it becomes difficult to fill up the card in time.

# Appendix

## ILO RECOMMENDATION NO. 150: RECOMMENDATION CONCERNING VOCATIONAL GUIDANCE AND VOCATIONAL TRAINING IN THE DEVELOPMENT OF HUMAN RESOURCES

The General Conference of the International Labour Organisation,

Having been convened at Geneva by the Governing Body of the International Labour Office, and having met in its Sixtieth Session on 4 June 1975, and

Considering the importance of vocational guidance and vocational training in the implementation of employment policies and programmes, and

Noting the terms of existing international labour Conventions and Recommendations of direct relevance to employment policy and, in particular, of the Discrimination (Employment and Occupation) Convention and Recommendation, 1958, and of the Employment Policy Convention and Recommendation, 1964, and

Noting that the General Conference of the United Nations Educational, Scientific and Cultural Organisation at its Eighteenth Session in 1974 adopted a Recommendation on Technical and Vocational Education, and

Noting that the International Labour Organisation and the United Nations Educational, Scientific and Cultural Organisation have collaborated closely with a view to ensuring that the instruments of the two

Organisations pursue harmonised objectives and avoid duplication and conflict, and that they will continue to collaborate closely with a view to the effective implementation of these instruments, and

Having decided upon the adoption of certain proposals with regard to human resources development: vocational guidance and vocational training, which is the sixth item on the agenda of the session, and

Having determined that these proposals shall take the form of a Recommendation,

adopts this twenty-third day of June of the year one thousand nine hundred and seventy-five, the following Recommendation, which may be cited as the Human Resources Development Recommendation, 1975:

## I

## GENERAL PROVISIONS

1. This Recommendation applies to the vocational guidance and vocational training of young persons and adults for all areas of economic, social and cultural life and at all levels of occupational skill and responsibility.

2. (1) For the purpose of this Recommendation, the qualification of the terms *guidance* and *training* by the term *vocational* means that guidance and training are directed to identifying and developing human capabilities for a productive and satisfying working life and, in conjunction with the different forms of education, to improve the ability of the individual to understand and, individually or collectively, to influence working conditions and the social environment.

(2) The definition contained in subparagraph (1) of this Paragraph applies to guidance, to initial and further training, and to retraining, whatever the way in which

they are provided and whatever the level of skill and responsibility.

3. In giving effect to this Recommendation, member States should take account of guidelines supplementing its provisions which may be formulated by regional conferences, industrial committees and meetings of experts or consultants convened by the International Labour Organisation and other competent bodies.

## II

## POLICIES AND PROGRAMMES

4. (1) Members should adopt and develop comprehensive and co-ordinated policies and programmes of vocational guidance and vocational training, closely linked with employment, in particular through public employment services.

   (2) These policies and programmes should take due account of—

   (*a*) employment needs, opportunities and problems, both regional and national;

   (*b*) the stage and level of economic, social and cultural development; and

   (*c*) the mutual relationships between human resources development and other economic, social and cultural objectives.

   (3) The policies and programmes should be pursued by methods that are appropriate to national conditions.

   (4) The policies and programmes should encourage and enable all persons, on an equal basis and without any discrimination whatsoever, to develop and use their capabilities for work in their own best interests and in accordance with their own aspirations, account being taken of the needs of society.

(5) Such policies and programmes should also encourage undertakings to accept responsibility for training workers in their employment. Undertakings should co-operate with the representatives of their workers when planning their training programmes and should ensure, as far as possible, that these programmes are in line with those of the public training system.

(6) Such policies and programmes should have as objectives—

(*a*) to ensure entry into productive employment, including self-employment, which corresponds to personal aptitudes and aspirations, and to facilitate occupational mobility;

(*b*) to promote and develop creativity, dynamism and initiative with a view to maintaining or increasing work effectiveness;

(*c*) to protect persons against unemployment or other loss of income or earning capacity deriving from lack of demand for their skills as well as against underemployment;

(*d*) to protect persons against excessive physical or mental strain in employment;

(*e*) to protect persons against occupational hazards by making high standards of teaching occupational safety and health an integral part of training for each trade or occupation;

(*f*) to assist persons in their quest for satisfaction at work, for individual achievement and self-expression, and for the betterment of their lot in life through their own efforts to improve the quality or modify the nature of their contribution to the economy;

(*g*) to achieve social, cultural and economic advancement and continuing adjustment to change, with the participation of all concerned in reshaping the work requirements;

(*h*) to achieve the full participation of all groups in society in the process of development and in sharing the benefits deriving from it.

5. (1) With the above ends in view, Members should establish and develop open, flexible and complementary systems of general, technical and vocational education, educational and vocational guidance and vocational training, whether these activities take place within the system of formal education or outside it.

(2) Members should aim in particular at—

(*a*) ensuring that all have equal access to vocational guidance and vocational training;

(*b*) providing, on a continuing basis, broadly conceived and realistic vocational guidance for the various groups of the population in all branches of economic activity;

(*c*) developing comprehensive systems of vocational training covering all aspects of productive work in all branches of economic activity;

(*d*) facilitating mobility between different lines of training, within and between the various occupations and sectors of economic activity and between different levels of responsibility;

(*e*) co-ordinating vocational training for one sector of the economy or branch of economic activity with vocational training for other sectors or branches;

(*f*) establishing patterns of systematic vocational training in all branches of economic activity and for all types of work and levels of skill and responsibility;

(*g*) providing all workers with real possibilities for re-entering the educational system, at a level which takes account of their work experience;

(*h*) establishing close co-operation and co-ordination between vocational guidance and vocational training provided outside the school system, on the one hand, and educational guidance and the school system, on the other;

(*i*) establishing conditions permitting workers to supplement their vocational training by trade union education given by their representative organisations;

(*j*) undertaking research and adapting administrative arrangements and methods as required for implementing the programmes of vocational guidance and vocational training.

6. The policies and programmes of vocational guidance and vocational training should—

(*a*) be co-ordinated with policies and major programmes of social and economic development such as employment promotion, social integration, rural development, development of crafts and industry, adaptation of methods and organisation of work to human requirements and improvement of working conditions;

(*b*) take account of international economic and technological interaction and co-operation;

(*c*) be reviewed periodically in relation to current and planned social and economic development;

(*d*) promote activities which will stimulate workers to contribute to improved international relations;

(*e*) contribute to fuller understanding of technical, scientific, economic, social and cultural matters;

(*f*) create and develop an appropriate infrastructure for providing adequate training respecting the essential standards of occupational health and safety.

## III

## VOCATIONAL GUIDANCE

7. (1) Members should gradually extend their systems of vocational guidance, including continuing employment information, with a view to ensuring that comprehensive information and the broadest possible guidance are available to all children, young persons and adults, including appropriate programmes for all handicapped and disabled persons.

(2) Such information and guidance should cover the choice of an occupation, vocational training and related educational opportunities, the employment situation and employment prospects, promotion prospects, conditions of work, safety and hygiene at work, and other aspects of working life in the various sectors of economic, social and cultural activity and at all levels of responsibility.

(3) The information and guidance should be supplemented by information on general aspects of collective agreements and of the rights and obligations of all concerned under labour law; this information should be provided in accordance with national law and practice, taking into account the respective functions and tasks of the workers' and employers' organisations concerned.

8. (1) The main objectives of vocational guidance programmes should be to—

(*a*) provide children and young persons not yet in the labour force with the basis for choosing a line of education or vocational training in the light of their aptitudes, abilities and interests and of employment opportunities;

(*b*) assist persons in programmes of education and vocational training to derive the maximum benefit from them and to prepare themselves either for supplementary education or vocational training or for entry into an occupation and for continuing education and training as and when required during their working lives;

(*c*) assist persons who are entering the labour force, who seek to change their work activities, or who are unemployed, to choose an occupation and to plan related education and vocational training;

(*d*) inform employed persons of opportunities for improving their occupational development potential, their level of performance, their earnings and their position, of the educational and vocational training requirements and of the facilities available for this purpose;

(*e*) promote general awareness of the contributions which are and can be made by the various sectors of the economy and branches of economic activity, including those which have traditionally enjoyed little prestige, to general development and to expanding employment;

(*f*) assist co-operating institutions to provide information and feedback on the effectiveness of particular training programmes as an integral part of vocational guidance.

(2) Members should ensure that such programmes are compatible with the right to freedom of choice in selecting an occupation and to fair promotion opportunities as well as the right to education.

9. In extending the scope of their systems of vocational guidance, Members should pay special attention to—

(*a*) helping children and young persons at school to gain an appreciation of the value and importance of work and an understanding of the world of work as well as to familiarise themselves with the conditions of work in as broad a range of occupations as possible—taking account of the employment and career opportunities that may be open to them—and with requirements for taking advantage of these opportunities;

(*b*) giving children and young persons who have never been to school, or who left school early, information on as broad a range of occupations as possible and on employment opportunities in these occupations, as well as guidance on how they may gain access to them;

(*c*) giving adults in employment, including self-employment, information on trends and objectives in development which concern them and in particular on the implications of social, technical and economic change for their field of work;

(*d*) giving unemployed and underemployed persons all the necessary information and guidance on possibilities of finding employment or improving their employment situation and on means available for achieving this purpose;

(*e*) giving persons who meet special problems in relation to education, vocational training or employment, assistance in overcoming them within over-all measures aiming at social progress.

10. (1) Both group vocational guidance programmes—namely the dissemination of factual material and counselling for groups of persons who have similar vocational needs—and individual counselling should be made available.

(2) Individual counselling should be available, in

particular, to young persons and adults requiring specialised assistance in identifying their occupational aptitudes, abilities and interests, in assessing the educational, vocational training and employment opportunities which are likely to be available to them, and in choosing a line of education, vocational training or employment.

(3) Individual counselling—and, as appropriate, group vocational guidance activities—should take into account the individual's specific need of information and support, with particular attention to the physically and mentally handicapped and disabled as well as to socially and educationally disadvantaged persons. They may include exercises in seeking and evaluating information and in decision making, as well as exposure to expanded career choices and goals, in order to develop the capacity to make an informed choice. They should always take into account the individual's right to make his own choice on the basis of comprehensive relevant information.

(4) Individual counselling should, whenever required, be supplemented by advice for remedial action and such other help as may be useful for the purposes of vocational adjustment.

11. Members whose vocational guidance programmes are in the early stages of development should, in the first instance, aim at—

(*a*) drawing the attention of young persons to the importance of choosing general and vocational education taking full account of existing employment prospects and of trends in economic and social development, as well as of their personal aptitudes and interests;

(*b*) assisting those groups of the population which require help in overcoming traditional restrictions on their free choice of education, vocational training or occupation;

(*c*) meeting the needs of those with special potential in fields of work which are of major importance.

12. Members should make full use, in their vocational guidance programmes, of all available facilities and media through which the various groups of the population concerned can be reached most effectively.

13. (1) Wherever practicable, appropriate tests of capacity and aptitude —including both physiological and psychological characteristics—and other methods of examination should be made available for use in vocational guidance as appropriate to the needs of individual cases.

(2) Such tests and other methods of examination should be used only in agreement with the person seeking guidance and in conjunction with other methods of exploring personal characteristics; they should be carried out only by specialists.

(3) The results obtained in the application of such tests and other methods of examination should not be communicated to a third person without the express agreement of the person examined.

14. (1) Where tests and other methods of examination are employed in vocational guidance, they should be standardised for the age groups, populations and cultures concerned and should be validated for the particular purposes for which they are intended.

(2) There should be a continuing programme for the development and restandardisation, at regular intervals, of such tests and other methods of examination in order to take account of changing conditions and life styles.

## IV

## VOCATIONAL TRAINING

**A. General Provisions**

15. (1) Members should gradually extend, adapt and harmonise the vocational training systems of their respective countries to meet the needs for vocational training throughout life of both young persons and adults in all sectors of the economy and branches of economic activity and at all levels of skill and responsibility.

(2) In doing so they should pay special attention to—

(*a*) providing opportunities for promotion which should be open, wherever possible, to persons with the desire and ability to reach higher levels of skill and responsibility;

(*b*) improving vocational training in sectors of the economy and branches of economic activity in which vocational training is largely unsystematic and in which obsolescent technologies and methods of work prevail;

(*c*) providing vocational training for members of the population who had not received adequate attention in the past, in particular for groups which are economically or socially disadvantaged;

(*d*) effectively co-ordinating general education and vocational training, theoretical practical instruction and initial and further training.

(3) Vocational training programmes should be so conceived as to promote full employment and the development of the capabilities of each person.

16. Vocational training programmes for individual occupations and branches of economic activity should, as

appropriate, be arranged in progressive stages which together provide adequate opportunities for—

(*a*) initial training for young persons and adults with little or no previous work experience;

(*b*) further training which should enable persons engaged in an occupation—

(*i*) to improve their performance or broaden the range of activities which they can undertake, to proceed to higher-level work or to gain promotion;

(ii) to update their knowledge and skills in the light of developments in the occupation concerned;

(*c*) retraining to enable adults to acquire new qualifications for a different occupational field;

(*d*) such further education as is necessary to complement the training;

(*e*) training in safety and health at the place of work, especially for young persons and adults with little previous work experience;

(*f*) acquiring information on rights and obligations in employment, including social security schemes.

17. (1) Every effort should be made to develop and utilise to the full, if necessary with public financing, existing and potential vocational training capacity, including the resources available in undertakings, in order to provide programmes of continuing vocational training.

(2) In the provision of training, advantage should be taken, as appropriate, of mass media, mobile units, and correspondence courses and other self-instruction programmes.

18. Programmes of initial training for young persons with little or no work experience should include in particular—

(*a*) general education which is co-ordinated with practical training and related theoretical instruction;

(*b*) basic training in knowledge and skills common to several related occupations which could be given by an educational or vocational training institution or in an undertaking either on or off the job;

(*c*) specialisation in directly usable knowledge and skills for employment opportunities which already exist or are to be created;

(*d*) supervised initiation into a real work situation.

19. (1) Full-time courses of initial training should, wherever possible, provide for adequate synchronisation between theoretical tuition in training institutions and training given on the job in undertakings in order to ensure that the former is related to the real work situation; similarly, practical training off the job should, as far as possible, be related to real work situations.

(2) Training on the job arranged as an integral part of courses given by training institutions should be planned jointly by the undertakings, institutions and workers' representatives concerned with a view to—

(*a*) enabling the trainees to apply in actual working conditions what they have learned off the job;

(*b*) providing training in aspects of the occupation which cannot be covered outside undertakings;

(*c*) familiarising young persons with little or no work experience with the requirements and conditions they are likely to encounter at work and with their responsibilities within a working group.

20. Persons entering employement after completing the full-time courses mentioned in Paragraph 19 above should receive—

(*a*) induction to familiarise them with the nature and objectives of the undertaking and the conditions in which work is performed there;

(*b*) systematic complementary training on the job, together with the necessary theoretical courses;

(*c*) as far as possible, planned experience in a series of activities and functions of training value, including adjustment to the workplace.

21. The competent authorities should, in line with national planning and national laws and regulations and after consultation of employers' and workers' organisations, establish national or regional further-training plans related to employment.

22. (1) Undertakings should, in consultation with workers' representatives, with the persons concerned and with those in charge of their work, establish and review at regular intervals further-training plans for persons in their employment at all levels of skill and responsibility; a joint committee may be established for the purpose.

(2) These plans should—

(*a*) provide opportunities to qualify for advancement to higher levels of skill and responsibility;

(*b*) cover technical and other training and work experience for the persons concerned;

(*c*) take account of the abilities and interests of the persons concerned as well as of work requirements.

(3) Persons in charge of the work of others should have an obligation to make an effective contribution to the success of further-training plans.

(4) Organisational responsibility for the establishment, implementation and review of further-training plans

should be clearly defined and should be assigned, as far as possible, to a special unit or to one or more persons operating at a level commensurate with such responsibility.

23. (1) Workers being trained within an undertaking should—

(*a*) receive adequate allowances or remuneration;

(*b*) be covered by the social security measures applicable to the regular workforce of the undertaking concerned.

(2) Workers receiving training off the job should be granted educational leave in accordance with the terms of the Paid Educational Leave Convention and Recommendation, 1974.

**B. Vocational Training Standards and Guidelines**

24. (1) Initial and further training leading to recognised occupational qualifications should be covered as far as possible by general standards set or approved by the competent body, after consultation with the employers' and workers' organisations concerned.

(2) These standards should indicate—

(*a*) the level of skills and knowledge required of candidates for the various vocational training courses;

(*b*) the level of performance to be attained in each major activity or function of the occupation concerned during each phase of training and, as far as possible, the content and duration of training and the facilities and equipment needed to ensure that the level of performance indicated may be attained;

(*c*) the part of the vocational training to be provided by the system of formal education, by vocational training institutions, by undertakings through trainning on the job, or by other means;

(*d*) the character and duration of any work experience that may be required in vocational training programmes;

(*e*) the training content, on the basis of the principles of multi-purpose training and occupational mobility;

(*f*) the methcdology to be applied, taking into account the objectives of the training and the characteristics of the trainees;

(*g*) any examinations to be taken or other means of assessing achievement;

(*h*) the certificates to be issued on successful completion of vocational training.

25. (1) The same occupation may be covered by more than one vocational training standard when, and for as long as, the conditions in which the work is carried out and the activities it involves vary widely between different sectors of the economy, branches of economic activity or undertakings of different sizes.

(2) Standards covering the same occupations should be co-ordinated in order to facilitate job mobility, with full recognition of the qualifications already held and of work experience in the occupation.

26. (1) Guidelines indicating the desirable organisation and content of vocational training should be established for occupations, levels of skill and knowledge and levels of responsibility for which the standards provided for in Paragraph 24 of this Recommendation are shown not to be appropriate.

(2) Such guidelines may be necessary in particular to cover—

(*a*) training for future supervisors, specialists and managers and for persons already employed in these capacities;

(*b*) training for training officers and for managers, supervisors and instructors of vocational training;

(*c*) vocational training for branches of economic activity in which there are large numbers of self-employed persons or of small undertakings;

(*d*) the improvement of vocational training for branches of economic activity in which there has been little or no provision for the necessary systematic vocational training, and for undertakings using obsolescent technologies and methods of work.

(3) Such guidelines may also be appropriate for the first training in employment of persons who have just completed full-time courses of initial training in educational and vocational training institutions.

27. Vocational training standards and guidelines should be evaluated and reviewed periodically, with the participation of employers' and workers' organisations, and adjusted to changing requirements, the periodicity of review being determined by the rate of change in the occupation concerned.

28. (1) Members should gradually establish standards and guidelines or, as the case may be, extend their applicability until all major occupations and all levels of skill and responsibility are covered.

(2) Priority should be given to vocational training for occupations and levels of skill and responsibility of key importance for social and economic advancement.

## V

## TRAINING FOR MANAGERS AND SELF-EMPLOYED PERSONS

29. (1) Training for management and supervisory functions should be provided for persons in charge of the work of others, for professional and specialist personnel participating in management and for persons being prepared to assume management and supervisory functions.

(2) The competent authorities should, in line with national planning and national laws and regulations and after consultation of employers' and workers' organisations, establish plans for training for management and supervisory functions and for self-employed persons.

30. (1) The content of programmes of training for management and supervisory functions should take account of the level of the current and prospective responsibilities of the trainees.

(2) The programmes should be designed in particular to—

(*a*) develop an adequate knowledge and understanding of the economic and social aspects of decision making;

(*b*) foster attitudes and abilities for leading and motivating other persons, while respecting human dignity, and for developing sound industrial relations;

(*c*) develop initiative and a positive attitude towards change and a capacity to appreciate the effect of change on other people;

(*d*) develop the capacity of assuming new responsibilities on the job;

(*e*) develop awareness of the importance of education, vocational guidance and vocational training for the personnel of the undertaking;

(*f*) develop awareness of the conditions of workers in their occupational life, concern for their welfare and knowledge of labour law and of social security schemes;

(*g*) develop understanding of the value of efforts towards self-improvement;

(*h*) provide the basis for further training in accordance with changing requirements.

31. (1) Vocational training programmes for self-employment should take account of the social situation of the worker and—

(*a*) include, in addition to training specific to the technical field concerned, training in the basic principles and practices of business management and of training other persons;

(*b*) develop awareness of the need to take initiatives and assess and accept risks.

(2) Such programmes should provide regular opportunities for updating training and be reinforced by a continuing flow of information on new developments in the technical field concerned, as well as on sources of finance and, if necessary, on the most efficient marketing methods.

## VI

## PROGRAMMES FOR PARTICULAR AREAS OR BRANCHES OF ECONOMIC ACTIVITY

32. (1) Appropriate programmes of vocational guidance and vocational training should be established for particular areas or branches of economic activity in which

comprehensive improvement action or major structural change is required.

(2) Such programmes should form part of national vocational guidance and vocational training programmes as a whole and be co-ordinated with other action to develop the area or branch of economic activity concerned.

33. Among the areas or branches of economic activity for which such programmes may be required, particular attention might be given to rural areas, to branches of economic activity using obsolescent technologies and methods of work, to industries and undertakings in decline or converting their activities, and to planned or newly established industries.

**A. Rural Areas**

34. (1) Programmes for rural areas should aim at achieving full equality of opportunity of the rural and urban populations as regards vocational guidance and vocational training.

(2) They should be conceived within the framework of national development policies, taking account among other things of patterns and trends in migration between rural and urban areas.

35. (1) Programmes for rural areas should make adequate provision for the special vocational guidance and vocational training needs of—

(*a*) agricultural workers, including plantation workers, small owner-occupiers, tenant farmers and sharecroppers and other persons engaged in agriculture and related activities, particularly in relation to agrarian reform and other major changes in supply, production and distribution systems in the areas concerned;

(*b*) persons engaged in non-agricultural occupations,

with special emphasis on education, communications, transport and other services and craft occupations.

(2) Such programmes should take account of differences in needs according to the type of rural activity involved, its degree of mechanisation, specialisation and modernisation and the scale on which it is conducted.

(3) Programmes for rural areas should include training in organising co-operatives and in managing undertakings.

36. (1) Countries in which facilities and programmes of vocational guidance and vocational training for rural areas are as yet little developed should concentrate initially on—

(*a*) providing information for young persons and adults in rural areas on the objectives of and action proposed for making improvements or major structural changes in the area and on the implications of such action for their work and lives;

(*b*) providing systematic education and vocational training, full time or part time as appropriate, for young persons in employment to complement informal learning on the job;

(*c*) providing short programmes of upgrading training or of retraining for adults through existing vocational training, or extension of other advisory services;

(*d*) developing social and economic leadership in rural areas and encouraging participation by broader groups of the population in development action;

(*e*) encouraging a desire for self-improvement.

(2) Such countries should keep their priorities for rural areas under review so as to work progressively towards—

(*a*) developing comprehensive vocational information and guidance services for the rural population as a whole;

(*b*) introducing or generalising systematic initial training for young persons;

(*c*) introducing comprehensive programmes of further training on a continuing or recurrent basis to meet the needs of adults.

37. Countries which, for financial reasons or lack of trained personnel, are not in a position to provide adequate services for the rural population as a whole, might consider—

(*a*) concentrating action temporarily on limited geographical areas where important lessons may be learnt for subsequent action in other areas;

(*b*) giving preference to landless labourers and other economically weak groups in rural areas, which are in greatest need of economic and social justice.

**B. Branches of Economic Activity Using Obsolescent Technologies and Methods of Work**

38. (1) Programmes for branches of economic activity and occupations in which the use of obsolescent technologies and methods of work is widespread should be developed as appropriate along similar lines to those for rural areas.

(2) The aim should be to provide vocational guidance and vocational training for persons employed in or entering these branches of economic activity or occupations which will enable them to participate in or contribute to the modernisation of methods and products and to benefit from changes introduced.

39. Extension and other advisory services for self-employed persons and small entrepreneurs in these branches of economic activity and occupations should provide them with information on possibilities of innovation in their work, and on related vocational training and other services.

40. In planning vocational training for such branches of economic activity and occupations particular consideration should be given to—

(*a*) needs and opportunities for extending the scope of or for specialising the activities of undertakings, and the vocational training implications of such extension or specialisation;

(*b*) possibilities of improving vocational training practices and, in particular, of providing opportunities for continuing training;

(*c*) possibilities of combining training services to managers of undertakings with other action for raising the level of performance;

(*d*) the creation of new opportunities for gainful employment.

41. Vocational training for such branches of economic activity and occupations—

(*a*) may be conceived initially as a complement to the learning systems by which work knowledge and skills are traditionally acquired;

(*b*) should take account of the needs both of young persons receiving initial training and of persons already working in these branches of economic activity and occupations, including the small entrepreneurs and other persons who give initial training to young persons.

### C. Industries and Undertakings in Decline or Converting Their Activities

42. When industries or undertakings begin to decline, workers affected should in good time receive vocational guidance and vocational training to facilitate a change in skills and provide the opportunity of finding new employment.

43. When industries or undertakings change their products and methods of production or the services they provide, workers affected should in good time receive training, organised in co-operation with the industries or undertakings concerned, to enable them to adapt themselves to their new tasks.

### D. New Industries

44. In planning vocational guidance and vocational training in connection with the establishment of new industries, account should be taken of—

(*a*) needs for workers, specialists, managers and administrators during the construction phase and after the new plants have been commissioned, and of any need for retraining persons employed during the construction phase with a view to placing them in other jobs after commissioning;

(*b*) needs for independent workers and entrepreneurs to undertake subcontracting for the new industries;

(*c*) the need to provide information relating to and vocational training for new activities rendered possible or necessary by the change in the economic conditions in the region;

(*d*) the need to provide vocational guidance and vocational retraining for persons whose knowledge and skills are rendered obsolete by changes in the structure of demand for labour within the region;

(*e*) the need to provide new opportunities for independent workers and entrepreneurs whose business may suffer from the competition created by the new industries.

## VII

## PARTICULAR GROUPS OF THE POPULATION

45. (1) Measures should be taken to provide effective and adequate vocational guidance and vocational training for particular groups of the population so that they will enjoy equality in employment and improved integration into society and the economy.

(2) Particular attention should be paid to such groups as—

(*a*) persons who have never been to school or who left school early;

(*b*) older workers;

(*c*) members of linguistic and other minority groups;

(*d*) handicapped and disabled persons.

### A. Persons Who Have Never Been to School or Who Left School Early

46. Measures should be taken to provide all persons who have never been to school or who left school before acquiring a general education adequate for integration into a modernising society and economy with vocational guidance, general education and training in basic skills, due account being taken of opportunities on the employment market.

47. Vocational guidance for persons who have never been to school or who left school before acquiring adequate literacy and numeracy should be as broadly conceived as possible, while taking account of special educational and vocational training facilities, and other opportunities for education, training and employment that may be expected

to be available to them.

48. (1) Arrangements for providing such persons with basic skills and general education might include—

(*a*) part-time instruction in knowledge and skills relevant to their work, and general education linked with that instruction, for children employed in the family farm or business or in other areas of the economy;

(*b*) courses in relevant basic skills and related general education for young persons and, if appropriate, adults, to facilitate their entry into systematic vocational training or to broaden their opportunities for employment and promotion;

(*c*) arrangements for special vocational training combined with productive work for young unemployed persons, supplemented as necessary by courses of general education, with a view to giving them such education, skills and work habits as are necessary for useful and remunerative economic activity;

(*d*) instruction in literacy and numeracy, particularly for adults which is linked with vocational training in the knowledge and skills required in a particular occupation or type of work and for active participation in development action; such instruction should be co-ordinated with general measures for the eradication of illiteracy;

(*e*) special educational and technical upgrading courses for young persons and adults in employment to raise the level of their performance or improve their opportunities for advancement;

(*f*) special courses in skills urgently required in employment for persons with little or no formal education.

(2) Special vocational training methodologies should be developed and applied for the arrangements provided for in this Paragraph.

49. The certificates obtainable through such arrangements should be co-ordinated with those obtainable in the system of formal education and by persons trained by other means.

**B. Older Workers**

50. (1) Measures to meet difficulties faced by older workers in employment might include as appropriate—

(*a*) identifying and changing as far as possible working conditions which are likely to accelerate the physical and mental processes of ageing;

(*b*) providing older workers with the vocational guidance and vocational training which they require, with special reference to any need for—

(*i*) updating their knowledge and skills by providing them with relevant information at the appropriate time;

(ii) upgrading the level of their general education and occupational qualifications by the use of specialists in adult vocational training, so that it may match that of better educated and trained young persons entering or already in the same occupation;

(iii) informing them at the appropriate time about facilities available for further training and carrying out such training at the appropriate moment, namely before the introduction of new working techniques and working methods;

(iv) making available to them, as appropriate, other positions in their own or in another occupation in which they can make use of their talents and experience, as far as possible without loss of earnings;

(v) ensuring that they are not debarred from vocational training by unrealistic age limits for admission;

(vi) developing a vocational training methodology adapted to the needs of older workers;

(vii) taking all necessary measures for the provision of technically and pedagogically competent instructors, well prepared to carry out further training adapted to the special requirements of older workers;

(*c*) encouraging older workers to take advantage of the vocational guidance and vocational training facilities or opportunities for transfer which will help them to overcome their problems;

(*d*) educating the general public, and particularly vocational guidance and vocational training staff, the staff of employment and other relevant social services, employers and workers, on the adjustments in employment which older workers may need to make and on the desirability of supporting them in such adjustments.

(2) Measures should also as far as possible be taken to develop work methods, tools and equipment adapted to the special requirements of older workers and to provide training in their use.

**C. Linguistic and Other Minority Groups**

51. Members of linguistic and other minority groups should be provided with vocational guidance which would inform them in their own language or in a language with which they are familiar, or if necessary through interpreters, of prevailing conditions and requirements in employment,

of the rights and obligations of all concerned and of assistance available for solving their particular problems.

52. Special vocational training programmes should be provided as necessary for linguistic and other minorities. In the case of linguistic minorities such training should, if possible, be given in the vernacular and should, as appropriate, include language training.

**D. Handicapped and Disabled Persons**

53. (1) Whenever they can benefit by it, persons who are handicapped or disabled should have access to vocational guidance and vocational training programmes provided for the general population.

(2) Where this is not desirable owing to the severity or the nature of the handicap or disablement or the needs of specific groups of handicapped or disabled persons, specially adjusted programmes should be provided.

(3) Every effort should be made to educate the general public, employers and workers, as well as medical and paramedical personnel and social workers, on the need for giving persons who are handicapped or disabled vocational guidance and vocational training which would enable them to find employment suitable to their needs, on the adjustments in employment which some of them may require and on the desirability of special support for them in their employment.

(4) Measures should be taken to ensure, as far as possible, the integration or reintegration of the handicapped and the disabled into productive life in a normal working environment.

(5) Account should be taken of the Vocational Rehabilitation (Disabled) Recommendation, 1955.

## VIII

## PROMOTION OF EQUALITY OF OPPORTUNITY OF WOMEN AND MEN IN TRAINING AND EMPLOYMENT

54. (1) Measures should be taken to promote equality of opportunity of women and men in employment and in society as a whole.

(2) These measures should form an integral part of all economic, social and cultural measures taken by governments for improving the employment situation of women and should include, as far as possible—

(*a*) educating the general public and in particular parents, teachers, vocational guidance and vocational training staff, the staff of employment and other social services, employers and workers, on the need for encouraging women and men to play an equal part in society and in the economy and for changing traditional attitudes regarding the work of women and men in the home and in working life;

(*b*) providing girls and women with vocational guidance on the same broad range of educational, vocational training and employment opportunities as boys and men, encouraging them to take full advantage of such opportunities and creating the conditions required for them to do so;

(*c*) promoting equality of access for girls and women to all streams of education and to vocational training for all types of occupations, including those which have been traditionally accessible only to boys and men, subject to the provisions of international labour Conventions and Recommendations;

(*d*) promoting further training for girls and women to ensure their personal development and advancement to skilled employment and posts of responsibility, and urging employers to provide them with the same opportunities of extending their work experience as offered to male workers with the same education and qualifications;

(*e*) providing day-care facilities and other services for children of different ages, in so far as possible, so that girls and women with family responsibilities have access to normal vocational training, as well as making special arrangements, for instance in the form of part-time or correspondence courses, vocational training programmes following a recurrent pattern or programmes using mass media;

(*f*) providing vocational training programmes for women above the normal age of entry into employment who wish to take up work for the first time or re-enter it after a period of absence.

55. Special vocational training arrangements and programmes, similar to those envisaged in clauses (*e*) and (*f*) of subparagraph (2) of Paragraph 54 of this Recommendation, should be available to men having analogous problems.

56. Account should be taken of the Employment Policy Convention and Recommendation, 1964, in the implementation of measures for the promotion of equality of opportunity of women and men in training and employment.

## IX

## MIGRANT WORKERS

57. Effective vocational guidance and vocational training should be provided for migrant workers, so that they will enjoy equality of opportunity in employment.

58. Vocational guidance and vocational training for migrant workers should take into account that they may have a limited knowledge of the language of the country of employment. Paragraphs 51 and 52 of this Recommendation should be applied to them.

59. Vocational guidance and vocational training of migrant workers should take account of—

(*a*) the needs of the country of employment;

(*b*) the possible reintegration of migrant workers into the economy of their country of origin.

60. Account should be taken, as regards vocational guidance and vocational training for migrant workers, of the relevant provisions of international labour Conventions and Recommendations concerned with such workers. These questions should also be the subject of agreements between countries of origin and countries of employment.

## X

## TRAINING OF STAFF FOR VOCATIONAL GUIDANCE AND VOCATIONAL TRAINING ACTIVITIES

61. Provision for the training of staff should cover all persons responsible either full time or part time for planning, organising, administering, developing, supervising or giving vocational guidance or vocational training.

62. (1) In addition to receiving training in vocational guidance, including individual counselling, persons giving vocational guidance should be familiarised with the world of work generally and with the conditions of work and functions of persons engaged in a broad range of occupations at all levels of skill and responsibility as well as with the employment and career opportunities in these occupations and

with the training courses and training facilities available for them; they should also be acquainted with general aspects of collective agreements and of rights and obligations under labour law.

(2) The training of persons giving vocational guidance should as appropriate include study of the physiological, psychological and sociological characteristics of different groups and of specialised guidance methods.

63. (1) Persons engaged in giving vocational training should have comprehensive theoretical and practical knowledge as well as substantial work experience in the technical field or functions concerned, together with technical and pedagogical training acquired in educational and training institutions.

(2) The training of such persons should, as appropriate, include study of the various characteristics and attitudes of different groups of trainees and of specialised training methods.

64. (1) Persons engaged in vocational training for particular branches of economic activity should be familiarised with the social, economic and technical aspects and conditions of the particular branch of economic activity concerned.

(2) For instance, in addition to technical and vocational education and vocational training in their speciality, persons engaged in rural development activities should receive training in such fields as—

(*a*) the economics of agriculture, forestry and other rural activities;

(*b*) methods and techniques of farm and forest management;

(*c*) rural sociology and institutions;

(*d*) mass communication and extension training techniques;

(*e*) the activities of co-operatives where such exist.

65. Persons engaged in vocational guidance and vocational training activities for particular groups of the population should be familiarised with the special social and economic problems of these groups.

66. (1) Persons responsible for planning, organising, administering or supervising vocational guidance or vocational training programmes, including directors and managers of vocational guidance or vocational training institutions or services, training directors and officers of undertakings, and vocational guidance and vocational training consultants, should have had experience of giving vocational guidance or vocational training respectively.

(2) Wherever possible, persons with such responsibilities in regard to vocational training programmes should have had experience of work in undertakings on other than vocational training duties.

67. All persons engaged in vocational guidance and vocational training activities should be given frequent opportunities of refreshing and updating their knowledge of social, economic, technical and psychological elements relevant to their line of work and of learning about new methods and techniques applicable to their work.

## XI

## RESEARCH

68. Members should make provision for research and experimental programmes designed with a view to—

(*a*) determining criteria for setting priorities and

establishing strategies for the development of vocational guidance and vocational training for particular branches of economic activity and groups of the population;

(*b*) determining and forecasting employment opportunities in the various branches of economic activity and occupations;

(*c*) increasing knowledge of the psychological, sociological and pedagogical aspects of vocational guidance and vocational training;

(*d*) evaluating the internal efficiency and external effectiveness of individual components of the systems of vocational guidance and vocational training;

(*e*) determining the direct and indirect costs and benefits of alternative patterns and methods of providing vocational guidance and vocational training;

(*f*) improving, for the population concerned, the psychological tests and other methods used for the identification of talent, the appraisal of aptitudes and interests, and the assessment of levels of knowledge and skill attained through vocational training;

(*g*) increasing available information on occupations and their requirements.

## XII

## ADMINISTRATIVE ASPECTS AND REPRESENTATIVE BODIES

69. (1) Public authorities and bodies concerned with general education and with vocational guidance, technical and vocational education, vocational training, training of staff for human resources development and management training, public authorities and bodies concerned with planning and implementation of employment and other social and economic

development policies, and bodies representative of the various branches of economic activity and occupations, and of the various groups of the population concerned, should collaborate in establishing policies, and in planning and implementing programmes for vocational guidance and vocational training.

(2) Representatives of employers' and workers' organisations should be included in the bodies responsible for governing publicly operated training institutions and for supervising their operation; where such bodies do not exist, representatives of employers' and workers' organisations should in other ways participate in the setting-up, management and supervision of such institutions.

70. In addition to participating in the establishment of policy and the planning and implementation of programmes, representative bodies should, subject to national laws and regulations and within the framework of national planning—

(*a*) encourage and assist their members to—

(*i*) provide opportunities and facilities for vocational guidance and vocational training;

(ii) support the provision of such opportunities and facilities;

(iii) make full use of them;

(*b*) provide vocational guidance and vocational training as necessary to complement the action of other bodies, services or persons and provide information which will facilitate such action;

(*c*) participate in research.

71. The respective roles and responsibilities of all those concerned with the development of human resources should be clearly defined.

72. In administering programmes of vocational guidance and vocational training provision should be made for—

(*a*) advising the bodies, services, institutions and undertakings concerned on the social, technical and methodological aspects involved in the implementation of the programmes;

(*b*) furnishing supporting services and facilities, such as research, standards and guidelines for the organisation of vocational guidance and vocational training and audio-visual aids and information on appropriate techniques and methods;

(*c*) organising publicly controlled examinations or applying other means of assessing achievement for occupations covered by vocational training standards;

(*d*) training of staff;

(*e*) making available research findings and other experience to persons or bodies responsible for planning and implementing the programmes;

(*f*) providing adequate financial support for implementing the programmes.

## XIII

## PERIODICAL REVIEWS

73. Members should periodically review programmes of vocational guidance and vocational training with a view to—

(*a*) achieving the best use of staff, facilities and media;

(*b*) adjusting the organisation, content and methods of vocational guidance and vocational training in the light of changing conditions and requirements in the various branches of economic activity and the needs of particular groups of the population, as well as in the light of advances in relevant knowledge;

(*c*) determining other action which may be required for the effectiveness of national policies for the furtherance of the goals referred to in Paragraphs 4 to 6 of this Recommendation.

## XIV

## INTERNATIONAL COOPERATION

74. Members should co-operate with each other to the fullest extent possible, with the participation, as desired, of governmental and non-governmental regional and international organisations, as well as non-governmental national organisations, in planning, elaborating and emplementing programmes of vocational guidance and vocational training.

75. Such co-operation may include—

(*a*) the provision, on a bilateral or multilateral basis, of assistance to other countries in the planning, elaboration or implementation of such programmes;

(*b*) the organisation of joint research and experiments with a view to improving the efficiency and effectiveness of the planning and implementation of programmes;

(*c*) making facilities available or establishing joint facilities to enable persons concerned with vocational guidance and vocational training to acquire knowledge, skill and experience which are not available in their own countries;

(*d*) the systematic exchange of information on vocational guidance and vocational training, including the results of research and experimental programmes, by means of expert meetings, seminars, study groups or exchange of publications;

(*e*) the progressive harmonisation of vocational training standards for the same occupation within a group of countries with a view to facilitating occupational mobility and access to training abroad;

(*f*) the preparation and dissemination of basic vocational guidance and vocational training material and aids, including curricula and job specifications, with a view to their use in a group of countries or a region with similar requirements or working towards the harmonisation of vocational training levels and of vocational guidance practices.

76. Members should consider establishing or contributing to the joint establishment or operation of centres for a region or group of countries to facilitate exchange of experience and promote co-operation in programme development and methodological research.

## XV

## EFFECT ON EARLIER RECOMMENDATIONS

77. (1) This Recommendation supersedes the Vocational Guidance Recommendation, 1949, the Vocational Training (Agriculture) Recommendation, 1956, and the Vocational Training Recommendation, 1962.

(2) The Vocational Rehabilitation (Disabled) Recommendation, 1955, the Vocational Training (Fishermen) Recommendation, 1966, the Special Youth Schemes Recommendation, 1970, and the Vocational Training (Seafarers) Recommendation, 1970, remain applicable to the categories of persons covered by their terms.

# Bibliography


Ash, P., "The reliability of psychiatric diagnoses." *Journal of Abnormal and Social Psychology,* 1949, 44/272-276.

Barnes, R K., Jr., "Through industrial therapy to self-sustaining jobs." *Employment Security Review,* 1954, *21* (9): 22-24.

Basham, J., Jones, A., and Messmer, P., Serving the severely disabled: mental illness. *Employment Security Review,* 1955, 22 (9):28-31.

Beers, C., *A Mind that Found Itself: An Autobiography.* New York: Doubleday, 1953.

Benson, J.P., Counseling teamwork in Delaware. *Employment Security Review,* 1955, *20* (9): 33.

Blain, D., Appel, K. E., Scheften, A. E., and Robinson, R. L., The current picture of mental health and psychiatry in the U.S.: pertinent statistics. *American Journal of Psychiatry,* 1955, *112:* 53-54.

Blos, Peter, *The Adolescent Personality,* pp. 43-58, 140-192, 209-213. New York: Appleton-Century-Crofts, Inc., 1941.

Braceland, F.J., Psychiatric lessons from World War II. *American Journal of Psychiatry,* 1947, 703/587-593;

Brennan, J. J., and Margolin, R.J., Utilizing community resources for the rehabilitation of psychiatric patients. *Personnel and Guidance Journal,* 1954, 32:330-335.

Brill, N. Q., Tate, Mildred C., and Menninger, W.C., Enlisted men discharged from the Army because of psychoneuroses; a follow-up study. *Journal of the American Medical Association,* 1945. 728:633-637.

Bureau of Labor Statistics, U.S. Department of Labor. *The*

*performance of physically impaired workers in manufacturing industries*. Bulletin No. 923. Washington: U.S. Government Printing Office, 1948.

Burgess, E.W., Social factors in the etiology and prevention of mental disorders. *Social Problems*, 1953, 1:53-56.

Cameron, N., *The psychology of behavior disorders*. Boston: Houghton Mifflin, 1947.

Cameron, N., and Magaret, Ann., *Behavior pathology*. Boston: Houghton Mifflin, 1951.

Cant, G., *New medicines for the mind, their meaning and promise*. Public Affairs Pamphlet No. 228. New York: Public Affairs Committee, 1955.

Carroll County, Iowa, "Curriculum Study," mimeographed report by L. A. Van Dyke, State University of Iowa, 1958.

Clark, D.A., and Vogel, V.H., Mental illness and the expanded federal-state vocational rehabilitation program. *Association for Research in Nervous and Mental Diseases, Proceedings* (1944), 1946, 25:292.

Clausen, J.A., and Kohn, M.L., The ecological approach to social psychiatry. *American Journal of Sociology*, 1954, 60/140-149.

Cobb, S., Contemporary problems in psychiatry. In *Theory and treatment of. the psychoses: some newer aspects*. Papers presented at the dedication of the Renard Hospital, St. Louis, October, 1955. St. Louis: Washington University, 1956.

Cohen, L., Vocational planning and mental illness. *Personnel and Guidance Journal*, 1955, 34:28-32.

Cunningham, J.M., Problems in the vocational rehabilitation of persons with psychiatric handicaps. *Journal of Rehabilitation*, 1946. 72 (5): 18-22.

Dael Wolfle, *America's Resources of Specialised Talent* (New York: Harper & Brothers, 1954).

Deutsch, A. Recent trends in mental hospital care. In: *Social Work in the current scene, 1950.* Selected papers, National Conference of Social Work. New York: Columbia University, 1950, pp. 143-159.

Deutsch, A., *The mentally ill in America,* New York: Columbia University Press, 1949.

Deutsch, A., *The shame of the states:* New York: Harcourt, 1948. 6. Fore, M. Opal. Experiment in the parole and hospital employment for the mentally ill in Iowa. *Mental Hygiene, N.Y.*, 1945, 29:423-428. 7.

Dunham, H.W., Some persistent problems in the epidemiology of mental disorder. *American Journal of Psychiatry,* 1953, *109:* 567-575.

Dunham, H.W., The current status of ecological research in mental disorder. *Social Forces,* 1947, 2.5/321-326. (In Rose, A. *Mental health and mental disorder: a sociological approach.* New York: Norton, 1955.

Dunham, H.W., The social personality of the catatonic-schizophrene. *American Journal of Sociology,* 1944, 49/ 508-518.

Eaton, J.W., and Well, R.J., *Culture and mental disorders.* Glencoe, Ill.: Free Press, 1954.

Edward C. Roeber, Glenn E. Smith, and Clifford R. Erickson, *Organisation and Administration of guidance Services* (New York: McGraw-Hill Book Company, 1955), p. 22.

Edward Carpenter, *Towards Democracy* (A. and C. Boni, New York, 1955) as quoted by Elliot and Klliot, *Solving Personal Problems,* Henry Holt and Co., New York, 1936, p. 196.

Elkin, F., Specialists interpret the case of Harry Holzer. *Journal of Abnormal and Social Psychology,* 1947, 42:99-111.

Elliot and Elliot, *Solving Personal Problems,* Henry Holt and Co., New York, 1936.

Erwin D. Stasek, "The Effects of Specialised Educational Counselling with Selected Groups of Underachievers at the Secondary School Level," unpublished Ph.D. dissertation, Northwestern University, 1955.

Eurich, Alvin C., and C. Gilbert Wrenn, "Appraisal of Student Characteristics and Needs," *Thirty-seventh Yearbook of the National Society for the Study of Education,* Part I, Chap. 2. Chicago: distributed by the University of Chicago Press, 1938.

Faris, R.E.L., Cultural isolation and the schizophrenic personality. *American Journal of Sociology,* 1934, 39:155-169.

Faris, R.E.L., and Dunham, H.W., *Mental disorders in urban areas.* Chicago: University of Chicago Press, 1939.

Felix, R. H., and Kramer, M., Extent of the problem of mental disorders. *Annals American Academy of Political and Social Science,* 1953, 286/5-14.

Fine, S.A., A structure of worker functions. *Personnel and Guidance Journal,* 1955, *34:66-74.*

Glenn E. Smith, *Principles and Practices of the Guidance Program* (New York: The Macmillan Company, 1951), p. 5.

Goldhamer, H., and Marshall, A.W., *Psychosis and civilisation.* Glencoe, Ill.: Free Press, 1953.

Greenblatt, M., York, R.H., and Brown, Esther L., *From custodial to therapeutic patient care in mental hospitals: Explorations in social treatment.* New York: Russell Sage Foundation, 1955.

Gustad, J.W., Inter-group problems in the development of rehabilitation counseling. *Journal of Counseling Psychology,* 1954, *1:243-246.*

H. Curtis Davis, "Where Does the Time Go?" *California Journal of Secondary Education,* October, 1953, 28:349.

H. H. Remmers and D. H. Remmler, *The American Teenager* (Indianapolis: The Bobbs-Merrill Company, 1957), p. 121.

Hamilton, K.W., *Counseling the handicapped in the rehabilitation process.* New York: Ronald, 1950.

Harold V. McAbee, "Time for the Job," *The Bulletin* of the NASSP, March, 1958, 42:41.

Henry B. McDaniel, with G.A., Shaftel, *Guidance in the Modern School*, New York: The Dryden Press, 1956.

Hoffman, H.H., "An evaluation of the first year of a parole clinic." *Hospital*, 1939, *13:87-92.*

House, J.W., and Marquit, Syvil, "Reactions of mental patients to attendance at a businessmen's luncheon dub." *Journal of Abnormal and Social Psychology*, 1950, 45:738-742.

Hunt, W.A., "A rationale for psychiatric selection." *American Psychologist*, 1955, 10:199-204.

Hunt, W.A., Wittson, C.L., and Hunt, Edna B. Hidden costs in the utilisation of the psychiatrically marginal man. *Journal of Clinical Psychology*, 1954, 70/91-92.

Ilgenfritz, W.O., "Interagency cooperation helps disabled veterans." *Employment Security Review*, 1954, 27 (9) :11-13, 24.

Israel, R.H., and Johnson, N.A., Discharge and readmission rates in 4254 consecutive first admissions of schizophrenia. *American Journal of Psychiatry*, 1955, 112:903-909.

J. W. Hedge and P.W. Hutson, "A Technique for Evaluating Guidance Activities," *School Review*, June, 1931, 39:508-19.

J. W. M. Rothney, *Guidance Practices and Results* (New York: Harper & Brothers, 1958).

J.G. Umstattd and Robert D. Thornton, "Secondary Education — Student Population," *Encyclopedia of Educational Research* (New York: The Macmillan Company, 1960), p. 1280. (Based on a study by Blyth C. Mitchel and Roger T. Lennon, World Book Company.)

Jaco, E. G., The social isolation hypothesis and schizophrenia. *American Sociological Review*, 1954, 19:567-577.

James B. Conant, *The American High School Today*, New York: McGraw-Hill Book Company, 1959.

Jersild, Arthur T., In *Search of Self: An Exploration of the Role of the School in Promoting Self-understanding.* New York: Teachers College, Columbia University, 1952.

Jones, M., The concept of a therapeutic community. *American Journal of Psychiatry,* 1956, 112:647-650.

Kenneth H. Hoyt, "Research Evidence of the Effectiveness of Guidance in Secondary Schools," unpublished paper, State University of Iowa, 1959.

Kohn, M.L., and Clausen, J.A., "Social isolation and schizophrenia." *American Sociological Review,* 1955, 20:265-273.

Kramer, M., *Facts needed to assess public health and social problems in the widespread use of the tranquilizing drugs.* Public Health Monograph No. 41. Washington, D.C.: U.S. Government Printing Office, 1956.

L.A. Van Dyke and K.B. Hoyt, *The Drop-Out Problem in Iowa High Schools,* State University of Iowa and Iowa State Department of Public Instruction, 1958.

L.J. Cantoni, "Reunion Party: An Unorthodox and Enjoyable Follow-Up of the Subjects of a 1939-43 Guidance Experiment," *Clearing House,* April, 1955, 29:466-69.

L.M. Terman, *The Intelligence of School Children* (Boston: Houghton Mifflin Company, 1919), pp. 80-81.

Lambert, G.F., "The counselor as a placement specialist." *Journal of Rehabilitation,* 1952, 78 (4):3-7, 29-30.

Landis, C., and Bolles, Marjorie, *Textbook of Abnormal Psychology.* Rev. ed. New York: Macmillan, 1950.

Landis, C., and Page, J. D., *Modern Society and Mental Disease.* New York: Rinehart, 1938.

LemKau, P. V., Tietze, C., and Cooper, Marcia, Mental hygiene problems in an urban District. *Mental Hygiene, N.Y.,* 1941, 25:624-646; 1942, 26:100-119, 275-288; 1943, 27:279-295.

Ling, T.M., Zausmer, D. M., and Hope, M., "Occupational rehabilitation of psychiatric cases: A follow-up study of 115 cases." *American Journal of Psychiatry,* 1952, *109:172-176.*

Lorr, M., Jenkins, R.L., and O'Connor, J.P., "Factors descriptive of psychopathology and behavior of hospitalised psychotics." *Journal of Abnormal and Social Psychology,* 1955, 50:78-86..

Lowrey, L., *Psychiatry for social workers* New York: Columbia University Press, 1943.

Martin, G.J., Reisman, M. J., and Noyes, A.P., Vocational rehabilitation in a psychiatric hospital: an initial report. *Mental Hygiene, N.Y.,* 1954, 38:107-112.

Mary Corcoran and R.J. Keller, *College Attendance of Minnesota High School Seniors,* Minneapolis: Bureau of Institutional Research, University of Minnesota, 1957.

Maslow, A.H., and Mittlemann, B., *Principles of abnormal psychology.* Rev. ed. New York: Harper, 1951.

Masserman, J.H., *Principles of dynamic psychiatry.* Philadelphia: Saunders, 1946.

Mehlman, B., The reliability of psychiatric diagnoses. *Journal of Abnormal and Social Psychology,* 1952, 47:577-578.

Menninger, W.C., Mental patients can be cured. *Reader's Digest,* 1956, August: 13-16.

Menninger, W.C., Psychiatric experience in the war, 1941-1946. *American Journal of Psychiatry,* 1947, 103:577-586.

Michael Serene, "An Experiment in Motivational Counselling," *Personnel and Guidance Journal,* February, 1953, 31:319-24.

Morris, Thais, and Stevenson, Ian. Psychiatry and social work in the vocational rehabilitation of psychiatric patients. In: *The Social Welfare Forum, 1953.* Official Proceedings, 80th Annual Meeting, National Conference of Social

Work, 1953. New York: Columbia University Press, 1953.

P.W. Hutson and A.D. Webster, "An Experiment in Educational and Vocational Guidance of Tenth Grade Students," Educational and Psychological Measurement, Spring 1943, 3:3-21. 208.

Patterson, C.H., "Matching versus randomisation in studies of counseling." *Journal of Counseling Psychology*, 1956, 3/262-271.

Phillips, J.C., and Mella, H., "Vocational rehabilitation of neuropsychiatric patients." *Occupations*, 1950, 28: 311-314.

Pratt, D., Re-employment of the psychoneurotic ex-soldier. *Psychiatry*, 1945, 8/3-8.

Rennie, T.A.C., and Woodward, L.E., *Mental health in modern society.* New York: Commonwealth Fund, 1948.

Rennie, T.A.C., Burling, T., and Woodward, L.E., *Vocational Rehabilitation of Psychiatric Patients.* New York: Commonwealth Fund, 1950.

Rennie, T. A. C., Burling, T., and Woodward, L.E., "Vocational rehabilitation of the psychiatrically disabled." *Mental Hygiene, N.Y.*, 1949, 33: 200-208.

Rennie, T.A.C, and Bozeman, Mary F., *Vocational Services for Psychiatric Clinic Patients.* Cambridge, Mass.: Harvard University Press, 1952.

Rennie, T.A.C., and Woodward, L.E., *Mental Health in Modern Society.* New York: Commonwealth Fund, 1948.

Rennie, T.A.C., and Woodward, L.E., "Rehabilitation of the psychiatric casualty." *Mental Hygiene, N.Y.*, 1945, 29: 32-45.

Robert E. Iffert, "Drop-Outs: Nature and Causes, Effects on Student, Family, and Society," *Current Issues in Higher Education*, Washington: National Education Association, 1950, pp. 94-102.

Robert J. Havighurst, *Developmental Tasks and Education* New York: Longmans, Green and Company, 1950.

Rockower, L.W., The development of a vocational-rehabilitation program for the neuropsychiatric. *Mental Hygiene, N.Y.*, 1949, 33:386-400.

Rogers, C.R., 'Client-centered therapy: a current view.' In Fromm-Reichmann, Frieda, and Moreno, J.L. (eds.). *Progress in Psychotherapy-1956*. New York: Grune & Stratton, 1956, pp. 199-209.

Rosanoff, A.J., *Manual of Psychiatry and Mental Hygiene* (7th ed.). New York: Wiley, 1938.

Roth, W.F., Jr., and Luton, F.H., The mental health program in Tennessee. *American Journal of Psychiatry*, 1943.

Rothney, John W.M., and Bert A. Roens, *Counseling the Individual Student*, New York: The Dryden Press, Inc., 1949.

Ruesch, J., and Bateson, G., *Communication: The Social Matrix of Psychiatry*. New York: Norton, 1951.

Sanderson, H., *Basic Concepts in Vocational Guidance*. New York: McGraw-Hill, 1954.

Schwartz, Charlotte G., *Rehabilitation of Mental Hospital Parents: Review of the Literature*. Public Health Monograph No. 17. Public Health Service, U.S. Department of Health, Education and Welfare. Washington, D.C.: U.S. Government Printing Office, 1953.

Scott, I.D., and Lindley, C.J., The advisement and guidance program of the Veterans Administration. *American Psychologist*, 1946, 1: 190-200.

Sinick, D., Placement's place in guidance and counseling. *Personnel and Guidance Journal*, 1955, 34: 37-40.

Sprol, S.J., The occupational adjustment of the psychoneurotic veteran. *Journal of Clinical Psychology*, 1948, 4: 264-269.

Stanley Caplan, "The Effect of Group Counselling on Junior High School Boys' Concept of Themselves in School,"

*Journal of Counselling Psychology*, Summer, 1957, 4:124-26.

Stantoch, A.H., Theoretical contribution to the concept of milieu therapy. In *Theory and treatment of the psychoses: some newer aspects.* Papers presented at the dedication of the Renard Hospital, St. Louis, October, 1955. St. Louis: Washington University, 1956.

Stanton, A.H., and Schwartz, M. S. *The mental hospital.* New York: Basic Books, 1954.

Steckel, H.A., The social service department and its relation to an extensive parole system. *Mental Hygiene, N.Y.*, 1922, 6:798-814.

Stephen Romine, "Youth Interests and the Educational Program of Secondary Schools," Bureau of High School Counselling and Accreditation, University of Colorado, 1951, p. 3-8.

Stevenson, G.S., Rehabilitation of the mentally handicapped. *American Journal of Psychiatry*, 1943, 700:289-290.

Strang, Ruth, *Counseling Technics in College and Secondary School*, rev. ed., Chap. 4. New York: Harper & Brothers, 1949.

Switzer, Mary E., Rehabilitation and mental handicaps. *Mental Hygiene, N.Y.*, 1946, 37:390-396.

Switzer, Mary E., Ten years of rehabilitation under Public Law 113. *Journal of Rehabilitation*, 1954, 20(4) :4-6, 26.

Switzer, Mary E., Vocational rehabilitation: a decade in review and a look ahead. *Employment Security Review*, 1954, 21(9): 8-10, 21.

Switzer, Mary, Rehabilitation and mental handicaps. *Mental Hygiene, N.Y.*, 1946, 37/390-396.

Taba, Hilda, and Deborah Elkins, *With Focus on Human Relations*, Washington: American Council on Education, 1950.

Tietze, C., Lemkau, P.V., and Cooper, Marcia, Schizophrenia, manic-depressive psychosis, and social-economic status. *American Journal of Sociology*, 1941, 4 7:167-175.

Unterberger, Hilda, and Olshansky, S.S., Vocational rehabilitation and the psychotic patient. *Journal of Rehabilitation*, 1955, 21 (1): 7-9.

Vogel, V.H., Psychiatric disabilities, including epilepsy and mental deficiency. In Kessler, H.H. (ed.) *The Principles and Practices of Rehabilitation*. Philadelphia: Lea and Febiger, 1950.

White, RW., *The Abnormal Personality*. (2d ed.). New York: Ronald, 1956.

Whitehouse, F A., "Vocational training in a rehabilitation center." *Journal of Rehabilitation*, 1951,17(1): 3-8.

Whitman, H., "Who are the insane?" *Woman's Home Companion*, April, 1952, 24027, 47.

Whitten, E.B., *Expanding rehabilitation programs*. (Editorial) *Journal of Rehabilitation*, 1955, 27 (3) :2.

Whitten, E.B., New Federal legislation for the handicapped. *Journal of Rehabilitation*, 1954, 20(6) :4-6.

Williams, R.H., *Psychiatric aspects of vocational rehabilitation—II. Institute for rehabilitation personnel held at the Menninger Foundation, November 16-20, 1953*. Bethesda, Md.: Public Heath Service, National Institutes of Health, Department of Health Education and Welfare, 1954. Mimeographed.

Williams, R.H., *Institute of vocational rehabilitation counselors. Teachers College, Columbia University, January 12-23, 1953.* Bethesda, Md.: Public Health Service, National Institutes of Health, U.S. Department of Health, Education and Welfare, 1953. Mimeographed.

Willis E. Dugan, "If I Were a School Administrator, This Is What I Would Look for and Expect from a School Counselor," *Epsilon Bulletin*, Phi Delta Kappa, State University of Iowa, 1960, 35:8-10.

Wittenborn, J.R., "Symptom patterns in a group of mental hospital patients." *Journal of Consulting Psychology*, 1951, *15:290*-302.

Wittenborn, J.R., and Holzberg, J.D., "The generality of psychiatric syndromes." *Journal of Consulting Psychology*, 1951, *15:* 372-380.

Wollaston, S.C., "Counseling teamwork in Massachusetts." *Employment Security Review*, 1953 20 (9) : 29-30.

# Index

## I



## J



## K



## L



## M



## N



## O



## P



## R

□□□